Writing Literature Reviews

A Guide for Students of the Social and Behavioral Sciences

SECOND EDITION

Jose L. Galvan

California State University, Los Angeles

 Pyrczak Publishing

P.O. Box 250430 • Glendale, CA 91225

Project Director: Monica Lopez.

Editorial assistance provided by Sharon Young, Brenda Koplin, Kenneth Ornburn, Erica Simmons, Randall R. Bruce, and Cheryl Alcorn.

Cover design by Robert Kibler and Larry Nichols.

Printed in the United States of America by Malloy, Inc.

"Pyrczak Publishing" is an imprint of Fred Pyrczak, Publisher, A California Corporation.

ISBN 1-884585-50-7

Contents

Detailed Contents

Notes:

Introduction to the Second Edition

It is important that students understand the steps involved in preparing literature reviews in the social and behavioral sciences. The primary focus is on reviewing original research published in academic journals and on its relationship to theoretical literature. However, most of the guidelines presented here can also be applied to reviews of other kinds of source materials.

Audience for This Book

This book was written for students who are required to "do library research" and write literature reviews as term papers in content-area classes in the social and behavioral sciences. Often, their previous training has not prepared them to search databases for reports of original research and related theoretical literature, analyze these particular types of literature, and synthesize them into a cohesive narrative. Instead, they are often taught how to use secondary sources such as encyclopedias, reports in the mass media, and books that synthesize the work of others. In addition, they are usually not taught the conventions for writing papers in the social and behavioral sciences. This book is designed to fill this gap by giving students detailed, step-by-step guidance on how to write reviews of primary source materials.

Students who are beginning to work on their theses and dissertations will also benefit from this book if they have not previously received instruction on how to prepare critical analyses of published research and the theories on which it is based. Undertaking a thesis or dissertation is stressful. This book should serve as a source of calm and logic as students begin to work on their literature review chapter.

Finally, those who are preparing to write literature reviews for possible publication in journals as well as those who need to include literature reviews in grant proposals will find most portions of this book helpful.

Unique Features

The following features make this book unique among textbooks designed to teach analytical writing:

- The book's focus is on writing critical reviews of original research.
- It guides students through a systematic, multistep writing process.
- The steps and guidelines are organized sequentially and illustrated with examples from a wide range of academic journals.
- Each chapter is designed to help students develop a set of specific products that will contribute toward a competent literature review.

Notes to the Instructor

Many colleges and universities have adopted a "writing-across-the-curriculum" program, in which all students are required to write papers in all courses. While the goals of such a program are admirable, many instructors are pressed for time to cover just the traditional content of their courses and have little time to teach writing. Such instructors will find this book useful because the explicit steps in the writing process are illustrated with examples throughout, which make it possible for students to use it largely on their own. In addition, many professors "naturally" write well but have given little thought and have no training in *how to teach writing*. Used as a supplement, this book solves that dilemma by providing a detailed guide to the writing process.

Much of what most of us know about writing was learned through what Kamhi-Stein (1997) calls the "one-shot writing assignment" (p. 52).[1] This is where the instructor gives an assignment at the beginning of the term, using the writing prompt, "Write a paper about *<specific topic>*." Conceptually, we tend to view this type of assignment as a single task, even though we may go through several discrete steps in the process of completing it. In fact, when writing papers that involve library research, the quality of the finished product depends in large measure on the care with which we undertake each of these steps.

In this book, the activities at the end of each chapter are designed to guide students through these various steps or stages of the writing process. These activities can be recast as a series of tasks that can easily be incorporated into the syllabus of a survey course in a specific discipline as a multistep writing assignment. Thus, this book has two complementary audiences: (a) instructors who may want to incorporate this multistep writing approach into their course syllabus and (b) students, working independently, who may need help in planning and implementing the various stages involved in completing a major writing assignment, such as the literature review chapter of a thesis or dissertation.

About the Second Edition

Many of the examples have been updated in this new edition. Also, two new sample literature reviews (A and D) have been added while Samples B and C have been retained from the First Edition.

Acknowledgments

I thank my supervisor, Dr. Theodore J. Crovello, for allowing me to

---

[1] Kamhi-Stein, L. D. (1997). Redesigning the writing assignment in general education courses. *College ESL, 7*(1), 49–61.

schedule days off when I need them and for encouraging me to find ways to continue to pursue my professional and academic interests, even while working as an academic administrator.

I am also indebted to my editor, Dr. Fred Pyrczak, for suggesting the topic for this book and for his generous assistance with the research design content of Chapters 1 and 5. In addition, I am indebted to my colleagues on the faculty of California State University, Los Angeles, especially Doctors Marguerite Ann Snow and Lia D. Kamhi-Stein, whose work on the multistep writing approach inspired this book's organization. All three of these individuals offered countless helpful suggestions, most of which are now part of the final manuscript. Errors and omissions, of course, remain my responsibility.

Feedback

I welcome your feedback and am especially interested in receiving suggestions that can be used to improve the next edition of this book. You can write to me care of the publisher using the address on the title page of this book or by e-mailing messages to me via Info@pyrczak.com.

Jose L. Galvan
Los Angeles, California

DEDICATION

For my daughter, Melisa,
a wonderfully creative and independent writer.

Notes:

NOTE: Theme issue topic: Montessori Foundations for Literacy and Culture
ERIC_ISSUE: CIJJUN2002

✔ Step 3:   Increase the size of your reference list, if necessary.

If you do not have enough references for your literature review assignment, you can, of course, search back further than the year 2000. In addition, you can search using some of the "major descriptors" and "minor descriptors" (also known as "keywords") found by clicking on the link in ERIC for each article (see Example 3.2.2 for the major and minor descriptors for reference 37 in Appendix B). Finally, once you have obtained the articles that seem most relevant, you should examine the reference list in each article. You will typically find references to additional articles that may be appropriate for use in your review.

ERIC classifies and makes available *educational documents* such as government reports, convention presentations, and printed material not normally available in libraries. This can provide additional references if you find you are short. For instance, a search for journal articles with the keyword "inhalants" from 2000 to the present identified only two articles. However, by not restricting the search to journal articles, ERIC identified 14 additional references to documents, including the one in Example 3.3.1, which is an unpublished teacher's guide. Such documents are identified with the letters "ED," followed by a six-digit reference number (in this case, ED447127). Large academic libraries maintain collections of these documents (usually on microfiche), making it possible to obtain them even though they are not published in the normal sense of the word.

Example 3.3.1

Sample information on an educational document identified through ERIC:

ERIC_NO: ED447127
TITLE: Mind over Matter: The Brain's Response to Drugs. Teacher's Guide. Revision.
PUBLICATION_DATE: 2000
ABSTRACT: This teacher's guide is for the "Mind Over Matter" series, a neuroscience education series designed to encourage students in grades 5–9 to learn about the biological effects of drug abuse on the body and the brain. "Mind Over Matter" includes eight colorful, glossy magazines, each of which is devoted to a specific drug or drug group (stimulants, hallucinogens, *inhalants*, marijuana, opiates, nicotine, methamphetamine, and steroids). Each of the magazines describes the effects of specific drugs or drug types on the anatomy and physiology of the brain and the body. These educational materials also highlight ways in which these drug-induced changes affect both behaviors and emotions. The background information and lesson plans contained in this guide, when used in combination with the magazines in the series, will promote an understanding of the physical reality of drug use, as well as curiosity about neuroscience. The guide presents background information on brain anatomy, nerve cells and neurotransmission, and the effects of drug abuse on the brain. It also suggests a brain anatomy educational activity that can be used throughout the curriculum as well as additional activities for each of the eight drug topics. Appendices offer resources, a reading list, and reproducibles. (SM)
MAJOR_DESCRIPTORS: Brain; Comprehensive School Health Education; Drug Abuse; Illegal Drug Use;

MINOR DESCRIPTORS: Biological Sciences; Elementary Secondary Education; Marijuana; Narcotics; Stimulants;
IDENTIFIERS: Amphetamines; Brain Functions; *Inhalants*; *Neurosciences; Nicotine; Steroids
PUBLICATION_TYPE: 055
PAGE: 61
CLEARINGHOUSE_NO: SP039610
AVAILABILITY: U.S. Department of Health and Human Services, National Institutes of Health, National Institute on Drug Abuse, Office of Science Policy and Communications, Science Policy Branch, 6001 Executive Boulevard, Room 5230 MSC 9591, Bethesda, MD 20892; Tel: 800-729-6686; Web site: http://www.sarasquest.org.
EDRS_PRICE: EDRS Price MF01/PC03 Plus Postage.
INSTITUTION_NAME: BBB10844 _ National Inst. on Drug Abuse (DHEW/PHS), Rockville, MD.
SPONSORING_AGENCY: BBB19417 _ National Institutes of Health (DHHS), Bethesda, MD.
CONTRACT_NO: N01 DA-3-2401
REPORT_NO: NIH-00-3592
LEVEL: 1
AUDIENCE: Practitioners; Teachers
LANGUAGE: English
GEOGRAPHIC_SOURCE: U.S.; Maryland
GOVERNMENT: Federal
ERIC_ISSUE: RIEAPR2001

Note that for a report to be published in a journal, it must pass the scrutiny of one or more editors and editorial consultants or reviewers with special knowledge of the area. This is *not* the case, however, for ERIC *documents*. ERIC does not attempt to judge the soundness or quality of the information in the documents. Thus, some documents may be less valid than journals as sources of information. Nevertheless, on most topics in education and related fields, you will probably find useful documents that can be used to lengthen your reference list.

✔ Step 4:   Write the first draft of your topic statement.

Now that you have identified appropriate references, you can reexamine the more focused list of articles you have generated and choose a more specific topic for your literature review. It is premature for you to decide on a final topic. You should do this only after reading some of the articles you have located. However, the first draft of your topic statement should attempt to name the area you will investigate. Think of this statement as a descriptive phrase rather than as a paper or chapter title. Example 3.4.1 presents two topic statements: one for a literature review in the area of linguistics and the other in psychology. Note that these first drafts are still very general. The remaining steps in this chapter will help you narrow down your topic statement.

Example 3.4.1

Linguistics:
Children's acquisition of features of language

Psychology:
The development of language and thought in children

✓ Step 5: Familiarize yourself with on-line databases.

All university libraries now subscribe to electronic databases. The manual searches of the past have given way to computerized searches. Therefore, it is essential that you familiarize yourself with your campus library's computer resources. If you are new to on-line databases, you should attend a workshop or class to learn how to use these services and pick up and carefully read all the handouts concerning your university's database resources. As noted earlier, this book will show you only how to approach databases in general—not all the specific features of any of them.

✓ Step 6: Identify the relevant databases in your field of study.

Every academic field has developed its own database services, which are used by its students and scholars. Early in your search, you should identify the databases specific to your field of study. In addition to the information you receive in the library, you should ask your adviser or instructor about the preferred databases in your major. Then, you can find out where they are available and whether they can be accessed from your home or dormitory.

Table 1 illustrates the range of database resources available through the California State University, Los Angeles (CSU, Los Angeles) library, as an example. This list is by no means exhaustive; in fact, larger research libraries will have many more research services than are listed in this table. If you are a student at a small university, it is recommended that you investigate whether your university's library maintains cooperative arrangements with larger institutions in your area.

Table 1
Summary of Selected Library Databases

Database	Subject Areas	Database Statistics
Basic Biosis	Life Science	300,000 records from 350 journals 1994–present, updated monthly
CINAHL	Nursing, Allied Health, Biomedical and Consumer Health	352,000 records from 900 journals 1982–present, updated quarterly
Dissertation Abstracts	Complete range of academic subjects	1,566,000 records 1861–present, updated monthly
ERIC	Education and related fields	956,000 records from journals, books, theses, and unpublished reports 1966–present, updated monthly

continued on next page

Table 1 continued

LLBA	Linguistics and Language Behavior Abstracts	250,000 records from journals, books, dissertations, book reviews, and other media 1973–present, updated quarterly
Medline	Nursing, Public Health, Pharmacy, Sports Medicine, Psychiatry, Dentistry, and Veterinary Medicine	9,305,000 records, including articles from 3,500 journals published internationally 1985–present, updated monthly
MLA	Literature, Language, Linguistics, and Folklore	1,308,000 records from 4,000 US and international journals 1963–present, updated monthly
NCJRS	Corrections, Drugs and Crime, Juvenile Justice, Law Enforcement, Statistics, and Victims	140,000 records, including journal articles, government documents, and unpublished reports 1970–present, updated periodically
PAIS International	Social Sciences, emphasis on contemporary social, economic, and political issues, and on public policy	451,000 records from journals 1972–present, updated monthly
PsycINFO	Psychology and related fields	1,249,000 records from 1,300 journals 1887–present, updated monthly
Social Sciences Abstracts	Sociology, Psychology, Anthropology, Geography, Economics, Political Science, and Law	562,000 records from 400 journals 1983–present, updated monthly
Social Work Abstracts	Social Work and related fields	30,000 records from journals 1977–present, updated quarterly
Sociological Abstracts	Sociology, Social Work, and other social sciences	519,000 records from 3,000 journals 1963–present, updated bimonthly
Sport Discus	Sports Medicine, Physical Education, Exercise, Physiology, Biomechanics, Psychology, Training, Coaching, and Nutrition	344,000 records 1970–present, updated quarterly

✔ Step 7: Familiarize yourself with the organization of the database.

The on-line databases described in Table 1 contain abstracts of several kinds of documents, including journal articles, books, conference presentations, project reports, and government documents. As you know from Chapter 1, this book focuses on reviewing articles in academic journals. For each of the thousands of journal articles in these databases, there is a single *record* with specific information about the article. In other words, each item on the list of titles you derive from your search of a database will be linked to an expanded description organized according to a set of categories of information. For instance, each of these records contains a number of *fields*, which include the article's title, author, source journal, publication date, abstract, and list of descriptors (i.e., terms and phrases that describe the article's contents). You can narrow the scope of a search by manipulating one or more of these fields. Publication date, source journal, and author are often used to narrow a search, but the most common method of searching a database is by specifying one or more descriptors. This method is covered next.

✓ Step 8: Begin with a general descriptor, and then limit the output.

Unless you have had previous knowledge of a particular topic, you should begin a search with a general descriptor from the database's thesaurus. If a thesaurus is not available, use a label or phrase that describes the topic you are investigating. If this procedure results in too many references, you can limit the search by adding additional descriptors using *and*. For example, if you search for "social" *and* "phobia," you will get only articles that mention *both* of these terms. Here is an example: Searching the major database in psychology, PsycINFO, from 2000 to the present yields 773 documents (mainly journal articles) relating to "phobia." A search for "social" *and* "phobia" for the same time period yields 484 documents. Finally, a search for "children," *and* "social," *and* "phobia" yields only 70 documents.

Another effective technique for limiting the number of documents retrieved from an electronic database is to limit the search to descriptors that appear in only the title and/or abstract (summary of the article), restrictions that are permitted in PsycINFO and some other databases. Using these restrictions will help to eliminate articles in which the descriptor is mentioned only in passing in the body of the article because an article dealing primarily with phobias would almost certainly mention the term in one of these important places. (Note that in an unrestricted search, the contents of entire documents are searched.) A search of PsycINFO restricting the search for "phobia" in only the titles and abstracts from 2000 to the present yields a total of 671 documents, which is about a hundred fewer than the 773 retrieved in an unrestricted search. With the additional restriction that "phobia" appears in *both* the title and abstract, 251 articles were obtained, which is considerably less than the original 773.

✓ Step 9: Use "on topic" records to refine the search.

As pointed out, the database's thesaurus is a good source of the key subject-matter terms used in that discipline, but another good source of more specific descriptors is a record from a previous search you conducted on a topic. In other words, once you find a record that deals specifically with your area of interest, you should review that record's descriptors for clues on how to further refine your search.

✓ Step 10: Redefine your topic more narrowly.

Selecting a reasonably narrow topic is essential if you are to defend your selection of a topic and write an effective review on it. Topics that are too broad will stretch your limits of energy and time—especially if you are writing a review for a term project in a one-semester class. A review of a topic that is too broad very likely will lead to a review that is superficial, jumps from area to area within the topic, and fails to demonstrate to your reader that you have thoroughly mastered the literature on the topic. Thus, at this point, you should consider redefining your topic more narrowly.

Example 3.10.1 presents a topic that is problematic for at least two reasons. First, it is much too broadly defined. Even though the writer has limited the review to English-speaking children as old as four years, it would be difficult to eliminate very many entries from Appendix B, leaving the writer with many more references than are needed. Second, this topic lacks a specific focus. Apparently, the writer has chosen to consider studies of children acquiring both the sound and the grammatical systems. If so, the finished review will either be a book-length manuscript (or two) or a superficial treatment of the literature.

Example 3.10.1
A topic that is too broad for most purposes:

This paper deals with child language acquisition. I will review the literature that deals with how children learn to speak in a naturalistic setting, starting with the earliest sounds and progressing to fully formed sentences. I will limit myself to English-speaking children, aged birth to four years.

Example 3.10.2 is an improved version of the topic. Note that this writer has narrowed the focus of the review to a specific aspect of language. The writer has stated clearly that the review has two main goals: (a) to catalog the range of verbal features that have been studied and (b) to describe what is known about the route children follow in acquiring them. Even though it is very likely that this topic will be modified several more times, based on the careful reading of the studies found, it is sufficiently focused to provide the writer with the basis for making a reasonable first cut of the studies in Appendix B.

Example 3.10.2
An improved topic description:

This paper describes what is known about how children acquire the ability to describe time and to make references to time, including the use of verbs and other features contained in the verb phrase. I will attempt, first, to describe the range of verb phrase features that have been studied, and second, to describe the path children follow as they develop greater linguistic competence with reference to time.

✔ Step 11:   Start with the most current articles, and work backwards.

The most effective way to begin a search in a field that is new to you is to start with the most current articles. If you judge a current article to be relevant to your topic, the article's reference list or bibliography will provide useful clues about how to pursue your review of the literature. In Appendix B, for example, a good strategy would be to obtain articles from the first two pages in the Appendix, photocopy the reference lists from the actual articles in the library, compare those lists against the contents of Appendix B, and make strategic decisions about rounding out your reading list. Keep in mind two important criteria for developing your reading list: (a) the reading list should represent the extent of knowledge about the topic and (b) it should provide a proper context for your own investigation if you are writing a literature review as part of an introduction to a research study you are conducting.

✔ Step 12:   Search for theoretical articles on your topic.

As you learned in Chapter 1, theoretical articles that relate directly to your topic should be included in your literature review. However, a typical search of the literature in the social and behavioral sciences will yield primarily original reports of empirical research because these types of documents dominate academic journals. If you have difficulty locating theoretical articles on your topic, include "theory" as one of your descriptors. A search of the PsycINFO database using the descriptors "social" *and* "phobia" *and* "theory" yielded 50 documents, including the one in Example 3.12.1, which would clearly be useful for someone planning to write about theories relating to social phobia.

Example 3.12.1

An article obtained by using the term "theory" in the search:

Chen, Y. P., Ehlers, A., Clark, D. M., & Mansell, W. (2002). Patients with generalized social phobia direct their attention away from faces. *Behaviour Research & Therapy, 40*, 677–687. [*Abstract*: This experiment tested whether patients with social phobia direct their attention to or away from faces with a range of emotional expressions. A modified dot probe paradigm measured whether [subjects] attended more to faces or to household objects. Twenty [subjects] with social phobia (mean age 35.2 yrs) were faster in identifying the probe when it occurred in the location of the household objects, regardless of whether the facial expressions were positive, neutral, or negative. In contrast, 20 controls (mean age 36.1 yrs) did not exhibit an attentional preference. The results are in line with *theories* of social phobia that emphasize the role of reduced processing of external social cues in maintaining social anxiety.]

It is important to note that writers of empirical research reports will often discuss the relationship of their studies to related theoretical literature and, of course, provide references to this literature. You should follow up these leads by looking up the references.

✔ Step 13: Look for "review" articles.

A corollary to the search technique described in the previous step is to use the descriptor "review" as a means of locating review articles. Previously published review articles are very useful in planning a new literature review because they are helpful in identifying the breadth and scope of the literature in a field of study. They usually will include a much more comprehensive reference list than is typical in a research article.

Note that some journals only publish literature reviews, some emphasize original reports of empirical research but occasionally will publish literature review articles by leading researchers in a field who seek to describe the "state of the art" in a particular topic, and others have editorial policies that prohibit publishing reviews. If you know the names of journals in your field that publish reviews, you might specify their names in a database search.[3] Because this will restrict your search to just those journals, this should be a separate search from your main one.

A search of PsycINFO using "substance abuse" *and* "treatment" as a keyword (descriptor) in any field *and* "review" as a descriptor in the *title only* identified 49 potentially useful articles that contain reviews on the treatment of substance abusers. Two are shown in Example 3.13.1.

Example 3.13.1

Two articles obtained by using "review" in the search:

Hopfer, C. J., Khuri, E., Crowley, T. J., & Hooks, S. (2002) Adolescent heroin use: A review of the descriptive and treatment literature. *Journal of Substance Abuse Treatment*, 2002, *23*, 231–237.

Leri, F., Bruneau, J., & Stewart, J. (2003). Understanding polydrug use: Review of heroin and cocaine co-use. *Addiction*, *98*, 7–22.

---

[3] In psychology, for example, *Psychological Bulletin* is an important journal devoted to literature reviews. A premier review journal in education is the *Review of Educational Research*.

✔ Step 14: Identify the landmark or classic studies and theorists.

Finally, it is important to identify the landmark studies and theorists on your topic (i.e., those of *historical importance* in developing an understanding of a topic or problem). Unfortunately, some students believe that this is an optional nicety. However, without at least a passing knowledge of landmark studies, you will not understand the present context for your chosen topic. If you are writing a thesis or dissertation, in which fairly exhaustive reviews are expected, a failure to reference the landmark studies might be regarded as a serious, if not fatal, flaw.

It is not always easy to identify historically important studies at the very beginning of a literature search. However, authors of some journal articles explicitly note these, as was done in Example 3.14.1.

Example 3.14.1[4]

Excerpt from a research article that identifies a landmark theorist and related studies:

A significant contribution of Rogers is that he was the first to attempt to demystify the nature of psychotherapy by making sessions open to public scrutiny. In the 1940s, he published verbatim transcripts of therapeutic encounters. For more than 50 years, investigators such as Porter (1943), Snyder (1945), and, more recently, Brodley (1994), using these transcripts, have measured how therapists actually behave with clients. Regarding this issue, Gill (personal communication, August 28, 1991) wrote, "I also think Rogers deserves a great deal of credit for being the first person to present verbatim sessions. Since him, a number of people have plucked up the courage to do so but he was the first." (p. 311)

While reading the articles you selected, you will often notice that certain authors' names are mentioned over and over. For example, if you read extensively on how social factors affect learning, you will probably find that Albert Bandura's social learning theory is cited by numerous authors of research articles. At this point, you would want to search the database again using Bandura's first and last names as one of the descriptors for two reasons: (1) to locate material he has written on his theory (keep in mind that you want it from the *original source* and not just someone else's paraphrase) and (2) to try to locate any early studies that he may have conducted that led him to the theory or that he originally presented to lend credence to the theory. Keep in mind that people who present theories very often conduct research and publish it in support of their theories. Their early studies that helped establish their theories are the ones that are most likely to be considered "landmark" or "classic." Note that when you conduct such a search of

---

[4] Kahn, E., & Rachman, A. W. (2000). Carl Rogers and Heinz Kohut: A historical perspective. *Psychoanalytic Psychology*, *17*, 294–312.

the database, you should *not* restrict the search to only articles published in recent years. Searching all years of the PsycINFO database while restricting the search to articles with the name "Albert Bandura" as the author of the article, *and* "social" in the title of the article, *and* "learning" in all fields yields relevant documents, including an early one, which is shown in Example 3.14.2.

Example 3.14.2

An early study by a leading researcher and theoretician:

Bandura, A. (1969). Social learning of moral judgments. *Journal of Personality and Social Psychology*, *11*, 275–279.

Finally, consult the textbook for your course. Textbook authors often briefly trace the history of thought on important topics and may well mention what they believe to be the classic studies.

Activities for Chapter 3

1. First, become familiar with the electronic databases in your field. (See Table 1 earlier in this chapter for a partial list of available databases.) You can do so either by attending a workshop in your university library or by reading the documentation and practicing on your own. Note that many libraries now allow you to search their databases on-line from your home, but you will probably need to use a university computer account to do so. Once you are familiar with the databases, select one to complete the following steps.

2. If your instructor has assigned a term paper on a specific topic, search the database using a simple phrase that describes this topic. If you are working on your own, select an area that interests you, and search the database using a simple phrase that describes your area of interest. How many sources did the search produce?

3. Retrieve two or three records from your search and locate the lists of descriptors. Compare the three lists and note the areas of commonality as well as difference.
   - Write down the exact wording of three descriptors that relate to your intended topic. You should choose descriptors that reflect your own personal interest in the topic.
   - Compared to the simple phrase you used when you started, do you think these descriptors are more specific or more general? Why?

4. Now use the descriptors you just located to modify the search.
   - First, modify the search to select more records.
   - Then, modify the search to select fewer records.
   - If you used the connector AND, did it result in more or fewer sources? Why do you think this happened?
   - If you used the connector OR, did it result in more or fewer sources? Why do you think this happened?

5. If necessary, narrow the search further until you have between 100–200 sources, and print out the search results.
   - Carefully scan the printed list to identify several possible subcategories.
   - Compare the new categories to your original topic.
   - Redefine your topic more narrowly, and identify the articles that pertain to your new topic. Prepare a typed list of these articles.

Notes:

Chapter 4

General Guidelines for Analyzing Literature

Now that you have identified the preliminary set of articles for your review, you should begin the process of analyzing them *prior to* beginning to write your review. This chapter is designed to help you through this process. The end result will be two important products: (a) a working draft of your reference list and (b) a set of note cards that will contain specific, detailed information about each article, both of which you will need before you begin to write.

✔ Guideline 1: Scan the articles to get an overview of each one.

Obviously, you read the titles of the articles when you selected them, and you probably also read the abstracts (i.e., summaries) that most journals include near the beginning of each article. Next, you should read the first few paragraphs of each article, where the author usually provides a general introduction to his or her problem area. This will give you a feel for the author's writing style as well as his or her general perspectives on the research problem. Then jump to the last paragraph before the heading "Method," which is usually the first major heading in the text of a research article. This is the paragraph in which it is traditional for researchers to state their specific hypotheses, research questions, or research purposes. Next, scan the rest of the article, noting all headings and subheadings. Scan the text in each subsection, but do not allow yourself to get caught up in the details or any points that seem difficult or confusing. Your purpose at this point is to get only an overview.

Example 4.1.1 shows in bold a typical set of major headings for a short report of original research in a journal article.

Example 4.1.1

Title [followed by researchers' names and their institutional affiliations]
Abstract [a summary of the complete report]
[An introduction in which related literature is reviewed follows the abstract; typically, there is *no* heading called "Introduction."]
Method
    Participants [or Subjects]
    Measures [or Measurement, Observation, or Instrumentation]

Results
Discussion [or Discussion, Conclusions, and Implications]

Longer articles will often contain additional headings such as *Assumptions*, *Definitions*, *Experimental Treatments*, *Limitations*, and so on. Scanning each of these sections will help prepare you to navigate when you begin to read the article in detail from beginning to end.

The last heading in a research article is usually called "Discussion" or "Discussion and Conclusions." Researchers often reiterate their major findings in the first few paragraphs under this heading. Reading them will help you when you read the results section in detail, which can be difficult if it contains numerous statistics.

Note that by following this guideline, you will be *pre-reading*, which is a technique widely recommended by reading specialists as the first step in reading a technical report. Because pre-reading gives you an overview of the purpose and contents of a report, it helps you keep your eye on the big picture as you subsequently work though the details of a research report from beginning to end. The information you gain by pre-reading will also help you group the articles into categories, as suggested in the next guideline.

✓ Guideline 2: Based on your overview (see Guideline 1), group the articles by categories.

Sort the articles you have amassed into stacks that correspond roughly to the categories of studies you will describe. You may choose to organize them in any number of ways, but the most common practice is to first organize them by topics and subtopics and then in chronological order within each subtopic. Example 4.2.1 shows a possible grouping of articles into categories and subcategories for a review of research literature on *affirmative action in higher education*.

Example 4.2.1[1]

I. Background Issues
      A. General Historical Background
      B. History of Affirmative Action in Higher Education
      C. Philosophical Basis
      D. The Law and Affirmative Action
II. The Effects of Affirmative Action
      A. Effects on Minority Enrollment

---

[1] This outline is patterned on Tierney, W. G. (1997). The parameters of affirmative action: Equity and excellence in the academy. *Review of Educational Research, 67*, 165–196.

B. Effects on Academic Achievement
C. Other Effects
III. Criticisms of Affirmative Action
IV. Alternatives to Affirmative Action

Organizing the articles into categories will facilitate your analysis if you read all the articles in each category/subcategory at about the same time. For instance, it will be easier to synthesize the literature on the effects of affirmative action on minority enrollment in higher education if all the articles on this topic are read together, starting with the most recent one.

✔ Guideline 3: Organize yourself before reading the articles.

It is important to organize yourself prior to beginning a detailed reading of the articles. You will need a computer, a pack of note cards to write your comments on, and several packs of self-adhesive flags that you can use to identify noteworthy comments. You can use different colored self-stick flags to mark different subtopics, different research methods, a review article or landmark study, or anything else that should be noted or might help you organize your review. If you are using a computer, you can use different colors of highlighting (available on modern word processing programs) instead of colored flags on note cards.

✔ Guideline 4: Use a consistent format in your notes.

Once you have organized the articles, you should begin to read them. As you read, summarize the important points and write them on the note cards.

Develop a format for recording your notes about the articles you will be reading, and use this same format consistently. Building consistency into your notes at this stage in the process will pay off later when you start to write the review. As has been noted, you will encounter considerable variation across studies, and your notes should be consistent and detailed enough for you to be able to describe both differences and similarities across them. Example 4.4.1 illustrates the recommended format for recording your notes. Remember to note the page numbers whenever you copy an author's words verbatim; direct quotations should always be accompanied by page numbers, and it will save you considerable time later in the process if you already have the page numbers noted. Make sure to double-check your quotes for accuracy.

Example 4.4.1
Author(s)' Last Name(s), Initial(s)
Title of Article

Publication Year
Name of Journal/Volume/Number/Page Numbers

Notes (*responding to the following questions*):
1. What is the main point of this article?
2. Describe the methodology used. (Include numbers of subjects, controls, treatments, etc.)
3. Describe the findings.
4. What, if anything, is notable about this article? (Is it a landmark study? Does it have flaws? Is it an experimental study? Is it qualitative or quantitative?, and so on.)
5. Note specific details you find especially relevant to the topic of your review. (Make this as long as necessary.)

The points in Example 4.4.1 are given as examples to guide you through this process. In an actual case, you may choose to disregard one or more of them, or you may decide that others are more appropriate. You may need to create several note cards per source. For example, you might have a card for each article on the main point of the article, another one on the research methodology used, and so on.

It may also be helpful to use a separate card on which you make note of questions or concerns you have as you read a particular article, or on which you note any conclusions you may reach about the subject of the research. These notes can later be incorporated into your paper, perhaps in your discussion or conclusion, and using a separate card for this will save you valuable time later.

Use paper clips or rubber bands to keep your cards on a given article together; this will help you avoid repeating the bibliographical details on every card.

✓ Guideline 5: Look for explicit definitions of key terms in the literature.

It should not surprise you that different researchers sometimes define key terms in different ways. If there are major differences of opinion on how the variables you will be writing about should be defined, you will want to make notes on the definitions. In fact, if several different definitions are offered, you might find it helpful to prepare a separate set of cards containing just the definitions.

To see the importance of how terms are defined, consider definitions of *justice programs* and *entertainment-based justice programs* in Example 4.5.1. It excludes programs that are more than one hour long and ones that are based on real events from the study. Another researcher who uses a definition without these exclusions might obtain different results. As a reviewer, you will want to note such differences in definitions since they may help explain discrepant results from study to study.

Example 4.5.1[2]

Considered a particular "genre," or general category of TV entertainment (Gitlin, 1979), "justice" programs (sometimes called police dramas, crime dramas, legal shows, or lawyer shows) were defined as half-hour or one-hour television programs that focus on some aspect of the criminal justice system, such as law enforcement, criminal prosecution, courts, or corrections. Furthermore, entertainment-based justice programs were defined as fictional; that is, characters and events are fictional, they do not portray real-life characters or actual events. Using these…definitions, the researcher discovered 13 entertainment-based justice programs being broadcast…which included: *NYPD Blue*…. (p. 18)

✓ Guideline 6: Look for methodological strengths.

It is unlikely that you will find a single research article with definitive results about any aspect of the human condition. Inevitably, some studies will be stronger than others, and these strengths should be noted in your review. Ask yourself how strong the evidence is, and keep in mind that in your role as the reviewer, you have the right and the responsibility to make these subjective evaluations.

The strength of an article may come from the methodology used. Do the research methods of one study improve on the data-gathering techniques of earlier studies? Does the article's strength derive from the size and generalizability of its subject pool? Does a set of studies demonstrate that the same conclusion can be reached by using a variety of methods? These and other similar questions will guide you in determining the strengths of particular studies.

As noted in Chapter 1, it is assumed that all students who take the time to read the literature carefully can make broad general assessments of the major strengths and weaknesses (see the next guideline) of empirical studies. For more advanced students, additional guidelines are presented in Chapter 5.

✓ Guideline 7: Look for methodological weaknesses.

Remember that you should note any major weaknesses you encounter when reviewing research literature. The same process you used in identifying strengths should be used when identifying weaknesses. For example, you should determine whether the author's research method has provided new insights into the research

---

[2] Soulliere, D. M. (2003). Prime-time murder: Presentations of murder on popular television justice programs. *Journal of Criminal Justice and Popular Culture, 10,* 12–38.

topic. Particularly, if an innovative methodology is used, does it seem appropriate, or does it raise the possibility of alternative explanations? Has an appropriate sample been used? Are the findings consistent with those of similar studies? Is enough evidence presented in the article for a reasonable person to judge whether the researcher's conclusions are valid?

Here again, it may be preferable to critique groups of studies together, especially if their flaws are similar. Generally, it is *inappropriate* to note each and every flaw in every study you review. Instead, note major weaknesses of individual studies, and keep your eye out for patterns of weaknesses across groups of studies. For example, if all the research reports on a subtopic you are reviewing are based on very small samples, you might note this fact on a separate card that relates to the collection of articles on that subtopic.

✓ Guideline 8: Distinguish between assertion and evidence.

A very common mistake made in literature reviews is to report an author's assertions as though they were findings. To avoid this mistake, make sure you have understood the author's evidence and its interpretation. A finding derives from the evidence presented; an assertion is the author's opinion.

In Example 4.8.1, readers can easily distinguish between the assertions in the body of the paragraph and the evidence-based statements in the last sentence. Bold italics have been added for emphasis.

Example 4.8.1[3]

The risk factor for binge eating that has received the most attention is dieting (Lowe, 1994). Dieting *is thought to* increase the risk that an individual will overeat to counteract the effects of caloric deprivation. Dieting *may* also promote binge eating because violating strict dietary rules can result in disinhibited eating (the abstinence–violation effect). Moreover, dieting entails a shift from a reliance on physiological cues to cognitive control over eating behaviors, which leaves the individual vulnerable to disinhibited eating when these cognitive processes are disrupted. In support of *these assertions*, dieting predicted binge eating onset in adolescent girls (Stice & Agras, 1998; Stice, Killen, Hayward, & Taylor, 1998), and acute caloric deprivation resulted in elevated binge eating in adult women (Agras & Telch, 1998; Telch & Agras, 1996). (p. 132)

---

[3] Stice, E., Presnell, K., & Spangler, D. (2002). Risk factors for binge eating onset in adolescent girls: A 2-year prospective investigation. *Health Psychology, 21,* 131–138.

✔ Guideline 9: Identify the major trends or patterns in the results of previous studies.

When you write your literature review, you will be responsible for pointing out major trends or patterns in the results reported in the research articles you review. This may take the form of a *generalization*, in which you generalize from the various articles, as was done in Example 4.9.1, which originally appeared in the last paragraph of a literature review article. Note that the references that support the generalization in the example were cited earlier in the review in which this excerpt appeared.

Example 4.9.1[4]

Of the nine interventions reviewed, the Arthritis Self-Help Course enjoys a well-established body of research supporting its efficacy and cost-effectiveness.... (p. 60)

Of course, you may not be as fortunate as the reviewer who wrote Example 4.9.1. There may be considerable inconsistencies in results from one research article to another. When this happens, you should try to make sense of them for your reader. For example, you might state a generalization based on a *majority* of the articles, or you might state a generalization based only on those articles you think have the strongest research methodology. Either option is acceptable as long as you clearly describe to your reader the basis for your generalization. Once again, careful note taking during the analysis stage will help you in this process.

✔ Guideline 10: Identify gaps in the literature.

It is every graduate student's dream to discover a significant gap in the literature, especially one that can form the crux of the student's thesis or dissertation study. In fact, gaps often exist because research in these areas presents considerable obstacles for researchers. These gaps should be noted in a literature review, along with discussions of why they exist. If you identify a gap that you believe should be addressed, make note of it, and take it into consideration as you plan the organization of your review, which is the subject of Chapter 6.

✔ Guideline 11: Identify relationships among studies.

As you read additional articles on your list, make note of any relationships that may exist among studies. For example, a landmark article may have spawned a new approach subsequently explored in additional studies conducted by others,

---

[4] Brady, T. J., Kruger, J., Helmick, C. G., Callahan, L. F., & Boutaugh, M. L. (2003). Intervention programs for arthritis and other rheumatic diseases. *Health Education & Behavior, 30*, 44–63.

or two articles may explore the same or a similar question but with different age groups or language groups. It is important to point out these relationships in your review. When you write, you probably will want to discuss related ones together.

✔ Guideline 12: Note how each reviewed article relates to your topic.

Try to keep your review focused on the topic you have chosen. It is inappropriate to include studies that bear no relationship to your area of study in your literature review. Therefore, your notes should include explicit references to the specific aspects of a study that relate to your topic.

If you determine that there is no literature with a direct bearing on one or more aspects of your research topic, it is permissible to review peripheral research, but this should be done cautiously. Pyrczak and Bruce (2003)[5] cite the example of year-round school schedules, which were implemented in Los Angeles as a curricular innovation, as shown in Example 4.12.1.

Example 4.12.1

When Los Angeles first started implementing year-round school schedules, for example, there was no published research on the topic. There was research, however, on traditional school-year programs in which children attended school in shifts, on the effects of the length of the school year on achievement, and on the effectiveness of summer school programs. Students who were writing theses and dissertations on the Los Angeles program had to cite such peripheral literature in order to demonstrate their ability to conduct a search of the literature and write a comprehensive, well-organized review of literature.

Such examples are rare, and you are advised to consult your instructor before you reach the conclusion that no studies have dealt with your specific research topic.

✔ Guideline 13: Evaluate your reference list for currency and for coverage.

When you have finished reading the articles you have collected, you should reevaluate your entire reference list once more to ensure that it is complete and up-to-date. A literature review should demonstrate that it represents the latest work done in the subject area. As a rule of thumb, use a five-year span from the present as a tentative limit of coverage, keeping in mind that you will extend further back when it is warranted. If your review is intended to present a historical overview of your topic, for example, you may have to reach well beyond the five-year span.

---

[5] Pyrczak, F., & Bruce, R. R. (2003). *Writing empirical research reports: A basic guide for students of the social and behavioral sciences.* Los Angeles: Pyrczak Publishing.

However, remember that the reader of a literature review expects that you have reported the most current research available. Thus, you should make explicit your reasons for including articles that are not current (e.g., Is it a landmark study? Does it present the only evidence available on a given topic? Does it help you to understand the evolution of a research technique?).

The question of how much literature is enough to include in a review is difficult to answer. In general, your first priority should be to establish that you have read the most current research available. Then, you should try to cover your topic as completely as necessary, not as completely as possible. Your instructor or faculty adviser can help you determine how much is enough.

Activities for Chapter 4

Directions: Refer to the printed list of sources you developed in Activity 5 at the end of Chapter 3.

1. Obtain copies of two articles from this list, and scan each of the articles.
   - Do the authors include a summary of the contents of the literature review at or near the beginning? If so, highlight or mark this summary for future reference.
   - Did the authors use subheadings?
   - Scan the paragraph(s) immediately preceding the heading "Method." Did the authors describe their hypotheses, research questions, or research purposes?
   - Without rereading any of the text of the article, write a brief statement describing what each article is about.

2. Based on your overview of all the articles on your list, make predictions of some of the likely categories and subcategories for your review. Reread the printed list of sources and try to group them by these categories and subcategories. Then, using these categories and subcategories, create an outline for describing the area of your topic.

3. Carefully review your outline and select the articles you will read first. Within each category, start with the earliest study and work toward the present. You now have your initial reading list.

Notes:

Chapter 5

Analyzing Literature from the Viewpoint of a Researcher

In the previous chapter, you were advised to make notes on important methodological strengths and weaknesses of the research articles you are reading prior to writing your literature review. This chapter will provide you with information on some points you may want to note regarding research methodology. Those of you who have taken a course in research methods will recognize that this chapter contains only a very brief overview of some of the important issues.

✓ Guideline 1: Note whether the research is quantitative or qualitative.

Because quantitative researchers reduce information to statistics such as averages, percentages, and so on, their research articles are easy to spot. If an article has a results section devoted mainly to the presentation of statistical data, it is a safe bet that it is quantitative. The quantitative approach to research has dominated the social and behavioral sciences throughout the 1900s, so for most topics, you are likely to locate many more articles reporting quantitative than qualitative research.

The literature on how to conduct quantitative research *emphasizes*:

1. Starting with one or more explicitly stated hypotheses that will remain unchanged throughout the study.[1] The hypotheses are reevaluated only after the data have been analyzed.
2. Selecting a random sample (like drawing names out of a hat) from a particular population, if possible.
3. Using a relatively large sample of participants (sometimes as many as 1,500 for a national survey).[2]
4. Measuring with instruments that can be scored objectively, such as multiple-choice achievement tests and forced-choice questionnaires, which participants

---

[1] Quantitative researchers sometimes start with specific research questions or purposes instead of a hypothesis.

[2] Even larger samples are sometimes used when large numbers of participants are readily available. Much smaller samples are sometimes used by quantitative researchers, especially when they lack the resources to study larger samples.

respond to by marking choices on a scale ranging from strongly agree to strongly disagree.

5. Presenting results using statistics and making inferences to the population from which the sample was drawn (i.e., inferring that what they found by studying a sample is similar to what they would have found if they had studied the whole population from which the sample was drawn).

Qualitative research also has a long tradition in the social and behavioral sciences, but has gained a large following in many applied fields only in recent decades. It is sometimes easy to spot because the titles of the articles often contain the word "qualitative." In addition, qualitative researchers usually identify their research as qualitative in their introductions as well as in other parts of their reports.[3] You can also identify qualitative research because the results sections will be presented in terms of a narrative describing themes and trends—often accompanied by quotations from the participants.

The literature on how to conduct qualitative research *emphasizes*:

1. Starting with a general problem without imposing rigid, specific purposes and hypotheses to guide the study. As data are collected on the problem, hypotheses may emerge, but they are subject to change as additional data are collected.

2. Selecting a purposive sample—not a random one. For example, a qualitative researcher may have access to some heroin addicts who attend a particular methadone clinic and may believe that these clients of the clinic might provide useful insights into the problems of recovering addicts.[4]

3. Using a relatively small sample—sometimes as small as one exemplary case such as a mathematics teacher who has received a national award for teaching (once again, a purposive sample—selecting someone who might be useful for obtaining important information).

4. Measuring with relatively unstructured instruments such as semistructured interviews, unstructured observations, etc.

5. Measuring intensively (e.g., spending extended periods of time with the participants to gain in-depth insights into the phenomena of interest).

6. Presenting results mainly or exclusively in words, with an emphasis on understanding the particular purposive sample studied and usually strongly de-emphasizing generalizations to larger populations.

As you can see by comparing the two lists above, the distinction between quantitative and qualitative research will be important when you evaluate studies for their strengths and weaknesses. For example, it is probably unfair to criticize a

---

[3] Note that quantitative researchers rarely explicitly state that their research is quantitative.

[4] Note that a quantitative researcher might also study the clients of just one particular clinic to which she or he happens to have access. However, in the quantitative tradition, use of a sample of convenience such as clients who just happen to be available (as opposed to a random sample from a larger population) would be viewed as a serious flaw.

qualitative study for using only one classroom of 25 students when the researcher spent six months in the classroom observing and interacting with the students, their parents, and the teacher to obtain detailed, in-depth information about them. (Note that it would be an exceptionally rare qualitative researcher who would have the resources to conduct such a study in hundreds of classrooms.) Still, you would want to make notes so that you can refer to the nature of this study in your literature review, as shown in Example 5.1.1. Notice that the reader has been informed that the study (a) is qualitative, (b) was intensive and long-term, and (c) involved only one classroom of 25 students. This is important background information for the readers, especially if you will be emphasizing the results of this study in your review.

Example 5.1.1
Portion of a statement in a literature review:

Of the four qualitative studies on teacher–learner interactions in the classroom, Smith (2004) presents the most intensive long-term study. In his study of 25 students in one classroom over a year, he found that….

On the other hand, a quantitative study in which forced-choice questionnaires mailed to all teachers in a large school district resulted in only 25 replies out of a potential 1,000 has a very important weakness because those who responded may be presumed to be a biased sample of the population (e.g., perhaps only those who were interested in the topic of the questionnaire responded), making any generalizations to the population of 1,000 very risky. Notice that this weakness in the quantitative study is not offset by some parallel strength such as obtaining detailed in-depth information by studying the 25 students intensively, as would be done in a qualitative study.

✓ Guideline 2: Note whether a study is experimental or nonexperimental.

An *experimental* study is one in which treatments are administered to participants *for the purposes of the study* and their effects are assessed. For example, in an experiment, some hyperactive students might be given Ritalin™ while others are given behavior therapy (such as systematic application of reward systems) in order to assess the relative effectiveness of the two treatments in reducing the number of classroom discipline problems. (Note that almost all experiments are quantitative.)

A *nonexperimental* study is one in which participants' traits are measured without attempting to change them. For example, hyperactive students might be interviewed to understand their perceptions of their own disruptive classroom behaviors without any attempt by the researcher to treat the students. Such a study might be quantitative (if the researcher uses highly structured interview questions with choices for students to select from and summarizes the results statistically) or qualitative (if a researcher uses semistructured or unstructured interview questions[5] and uses words to summarize the results in terms of themes, models, or theories).

Here is an important caveat: Do not fall into the bad habit of referring to all empirical studies as experiments. For example, if you are reviewing nonexperimental studies, refer to them as "studies"—not "experiments." Use the term "experiment" only if treatments were administered to participants in order to observe the effects of the treatments.

✔ Guideline 3:   In an experiment, note whether the participants were assigned at random to treatment conditions.

An experiment in which participants are assigned at random to treatments is known as a *true experiment*. Random assignment guarantees that there is no bias in the assignment (i.e., with random assignment, there is no bias that would systematically assign the more disruptive students to the behavior therapy treatment while assigning the rest to be treated with Ritalin™). Other things being equal, more weight should be given to true experiments than to experiments using other methods of assignment such as using the students in one school as the experimental group and the students in another school as the control group. Note that students are not assigned schools at random. Hence, there may be important preexisting differences between the students in the two schools, which may confound the interpretation of the results of such an experiment (e.g., socioeconomic status, language background, or self-selection, as occurs in "magnet" schools for the arts, the sciences, etc.).

✔ Guideline 4:   Note attempts to examine cause-and-effect issues in nonexperimental studies.

The experimental method (with random assignment to treatment conditions) is widely regarded as the best quantitative method for investigating cause-and-effect issues. However, it is sometimes unethical, illegal, or administratively unfeasible to treat participants in certain ways. For example, if a researcher was exploring a possible causal link between the divorce of parents and their children dropping out of high school, it would be unethical to force some parents to get divorced while forcing others to remain married for the purposes of an experiment. For this research problem, the best that can be done is to obtain some students who have dropped out and some who have not dropped out but who

---

[5] In addition, a qualitative researcher would be likely to conduct significantly longer interviews and, possibly, more than one interview.

are very similar in other important respects (such as socioeconomic status, the quality of the schools they attended, and so on) and then check to see if their parents' divorce rates differ in the hypothesized direction.[6] Suppose that the children of the divorced parents had somewhat higher drop-out rates than those of the children of nondivorced parents. Does this mean that divorce causes higher drop-out rates? Not necessarily. The conclusion is debatable because the researchers may have overlooked a number of other possible causal variables. Here is just one: Perhaps parents who tend to get divorced have poorer interpersonal skills and relate less well to their children. It may be this deficit in the children's upbringing (and not the divorce *per se*) that contributed to dropping out.[7]

The study we are considering is an example of a causal-comparative (or *ex post facto*) study. When using it, a researcher observes a current condition or outcome (such as dropping out) and searches the past for possible causal variables (such as divorce). Because causal-comparative studies are considered to be more prone to error than true experiments for examining causality, you should note when a conclusion is based on the causal-comparative method. In addition, you should consider whether there are other plausible causal interpretations the researcher may have overlooked.

✓ Guideline 5: Note how the major variables were measured.

Most researchers directly address the issues of whether their measures are valid (i.e., measure what they claim to measure) and reliable (i.e., yield consistent results) in their research reports. However, many of them provide only brief information on these issues in their research reports. When they are brief, they often refer readers to other published sources of information on these characteristics of the measures they have used.[8] Other researchers provide extensive information on these matters, especially when they have used new measures designed for the research study on which they are reporting.

In either case, you should attempt to make preliminary assessments of whether the measures used seem appropriate for the research purpose. In addition,

---

[6] If the researcher had considerable resources and a long time frame, a prospective study could be conducted in which children are followed from the time they start school until they finish school, noting who drops out and who does not drop out as well as whose parents got divorced. This method is also inferior to the experimental method for identifying cause-and-effect relationships because of possible confounding variables (i.e., many variables other than divorce may be responsible for the dropping-out behavior, and the researchers may fail to control for them all).

[7] If this limitation is still not clear, consider the example further. Suppose that based on the study in question, a dictatorial government made it illegal for parents to divorce in order to reduce the dropout rate. If the real cause of dropping out was parents' poor interpersonal skills, preventing divorce would not have the presumed effect since it was misidentified as a causal agent. Instead, the government should have mounted programs to assist parents to improve their interpersonal skills, especially in dealing with their children.

[8] Note that quantitative researchers tend to call their measures "instruments."

you should make notes on the types of measures used. This will allow you to make additional judgments when you review your notes in preparation for writing your literature review. As a general principle, if various researchers have used different methods of observation (e.g., questionnaires, observations, and interviews) and reached similar conclusions, these conclusions should be regarded as stronger than conclusions based on various studies in which all the researchers used the same method of measurement.

Your notes might also reveal certain patterns that shed some light on discrepancies in results obtained by various researchers. For example, do all the studies that support a certain conclusion use one method of measurement while those that support a different conclusion use a different method? If your notes revealed this, you might consider making a statement such as the one in Example 5.5.1.

Example 5.5.1

A statement from a literature review that points out differences in measurement techniques (desirable):

While the two studies that used mailed questionnaires support the finding that inhalant use among adolescents is extremely rare (less than one-half of 1%), the three studies that used face-to-face interviews reported an incidence of more than 5%.

Note that Example 5.5.1 is much more informative than Example 5.5.2.

Example 5.5.2

A statement from a literature review that fails to point out differences in measurement techniques (undesirable):

The research on the incidence of adolescent inhalant use has yielded mixed results, with two studies reporting that it is extremely rare and three others reporting an incidence of more than 5%.

✔ Guideline 6: Note the characteristics of the samples of participants.

As you learned in the first guideline in this chapter, quantitative and qualitative researchers have different perspectives on the selection of samples of participants. Without taking sides, it seems safe to say that if you plan to make generalizations in your literature review, you should make notes on whether the samples studied are likely to be representative of the populations to which one might wish to generalize. From quantitative researchers' points of view, random samples are best for this purpose.

Chapter 8

Guidelines for Developing a Coherent Essay

This chapter is designed to help you refine your first draft by guiding you in developing a coherent essay. Remember that a literature review should not be written as a series of connected summaries (or annotations) of the several articles you have read. Instead, the review should have a clearly stated argument, and it should be developed in such a way that all of its elements work together to communicate a well-reasoned account of that argument.

✓ Guideline 1: Describe the outline of your review for the reader.

An effective literature review is often a synthesis of research from more than one specific field or area of study. In other words, you can fairly well predict that your readers will be unfamiliar with some of the work you will cover, even if they are from your discipline area. However, even if they are familiar with the literature, your synthesis will be providing a unique interpretation, which your readers should be able to grasp quickly. For these reasons, it is important in academic writing to provide your readers with an explicit road map of your argument. This is usually done in the introductory section of the review, which should include an overview of what will be covered in the rest of the document. Example 8.1.1 illustrates this.

Example 8.1.1[1]

An effective "road map" at the beginning of a review:

Given the adverse outcomes they expose themselves to by delaying and failing to act, why do humans so frequently engage in decision avoidance? Herein I consider a variety of choice behaviors as reflections of an individual's underlying decision avoidance, a pattern of behavior in which individuals seek to avoid the responsibility of making a decision by delaying or choosing options they perceive to be nondecisions. This review reveals that in all such cases, there is a mixture of a few good, rational reasons for avoidance and a more complex and rationally questionable role played by emotions such as regret and fear. These issues form the basis of this article: (a) the delineation of boundary conditions under which persons

---

[1] Anderson, C. J. (2003). The psychology of doing nothing: Forms of decision avoidance result from reason and emotion. *Psychological Bulletin*, *129*, 139–167.

73

hesitate, defer, or choose options that require no action on their part or no change to the status quo and (b) the explanation for that behavior. (p. 139)

✔ Guideline 2:   Near the beginning of a review, state explicitly what will and will not be covered.

Some topics are so broad that it will not be possible for you to cover the research completely in your review, especially if you are writing a term paper, which may have page-length restrictions imposed by your instructor, or an article for publication, in which reviews traditionally are relatively short. In such cases, you should state explicitly, near the beginning of your review, what will and will not be covered (i.e., the delimitations of your review). The excerpt in Example 8.2.1 illustrates application of this guideline. Note that the reviewers first provide a definition and indicate that their review includes *deceiving* and *lying* (as being interchangeable). They then state that the review will be limited by two criteria.

Example 8.2.1[2]

A statement of the delimitations of a review:

We define deception as a deliberate attempt to mislead others. Falsehoods communicated by people who are mistaken or self-deceived are not lies, but literal truths designed to mislead are lies. Although some scholars draw a distinction between *deceiving* and *lying* (e.g., Bok, 1978), we use the terms interchangeably. As Zuckerman et al. (1981) did in their review, we limit our analysis to behaviors that can be discerned by human perceivers without the aid of any special equipment. We also limit our review to studies of adults, as the dynamics of deceiving may be markedly different in children (e.g., Feldman, Devin-Sheehan, & Allen, 1978; Lewis, Stanger, & Sullivan, 1989; Shennum & Bugental, 1982). (p. 74)

✔ Guideline 3:   Specify your point of view early in the review.

As has been emphasized previously, your literature review should be written in the form of an essay that has a particular point of view in looking at the reviewed research. This point of view serves as the thesis statement of your essay (the assertion or proposition that is supported in the remainder of the essay).

The expression of your point of view does not need to be elaborate or detailed (although it can be). In Example 8.3.1, the reviewers briefly indicate their point of view (that SES, cognitive–emotional factors, and health may be dynamically linked). This informs readers very early in the review that this overarching point of view guides the interpretation and synthesis of the literature.

---

[2] DePaulo, B. M. et al. (2003). Cues to deception. *Psychological Bulletin, 129,* 74–118.

Of course, you should settle on a point of view only *after* you have read and considered the body of literature as a whole. In other words, this guideline indicates when you should *express* your point of view (early in the review), not when you should develop a point of view.

Example 8.3.1[3]

Early summary of the path of an argument:

The associations between SES and cognitive–emotional factors have not been presented in any recent, enumerative reviews (but see the review of SES and psychiatric disorders by Kohn, Dohrenwend, & Mirotznik, 1998), and we therefore analyze this research in more detail. Following our review and critical analysis, we present a framework for understanding the pathways that may dynamically link SES, cognitive–emotional factors, and health. Finally, we conclude with recommendations for future research to better address the proposed mediation hypothesis. (p. 14)

✓ Guideline 4: Aim for a clear and cohesive essay; avoid annotations.

It has been emphasized several times thus far that an effective literature review should be written in the form of an essay. Perhaps the single most reported problem for novice academic writers is their difficulty in abandoning the use of annotations in the body of a literature review.

Annotations are brief summaries of the contents of articles. Stringing together several annotations in the body of a review may describe what research is available on a topic, but it fails to organize the material for the reader. An effective review of literature is organized to make a point. The writer needs to describe how the individual studies relate to one another. What are the relative strengths and weaknesses? Where are the gaps, and why do they exist? All these details and more need to support the author's main purpose for writing the review. The detailed outline developed in Chapter 6 describes the path of the argument, but it is up to the writer to translate this into a prose account that integrates the important details of the research literature into an essay that communicates a point of view.

Example 8.4.1 shows how a number of studies can be cited together as part of a single paragraph. The paragraph starts with a topic sentence and ends with an elaboration on the topic sentence based on the citations from the literature within the paragraph. Note that one of the points made by the reviewers is supported by three references. Clearly, then, the organization of the paragraph is topical—not around the reports of individual authors.

---

[3] Gallo, L. C., & Matthews, K. A. (2003). Understanding the association between socioeconomic status and physical health: Do negative emotions play a role? *Psychological Bulletin, 129*, 10–51.

Example 8.4.1[4]

A single paragraph with multiple sources:

At the family level, the nature of relationships between parents and children could play a role in asthma hospitalizations. Children with asthma have been found to have higher rates of clinically significant family stress as compared with healthy children (Bussing, Burket, & Kelleher, 1996). Children whose families are more cohesive are more likely to have controlled rather than uncontrolled asthma (Meijer, Griffioen, van Nierop, & Oppenheimer, 1995). Additionally, parenting difficulties early in a child's life, particularly during times of high stress, have been found to predict the onset of asthma in childhood (Klinnert, Mrazek, & Mrazek, 1994; Klinnert et al., 2001; Mrazek et al., 1999). Thus, strain in the family, in terms of both conflicts among family members and impact of illness on family relationships, could be associated with more frequent hospitalizations among children with asthma. (p. 14)

✓ Guideline 5:   Use subheadings, especially in long reviews.

Because long reviews, especially those written for theses and dissertations, often deal with articles from more than one discipline area, it is advisable to use subheadings. If you decide to use subheadings, place them strategically to help advance your argument and allow the reader to follow your discussion more easily. The topic outline you prepared in Chapter 6 can help you to determine where they should be placed, though you may need to recast some of the topic headings as labels rather than statements.

✓ Guideline 6:   Use transitions to help trace your argument.

Strategic transitional phrases can help readers follow your argument. For instance, you can use transitions to provide readers with textual clues that mark the progression of a discussion, such as when you begin paragraphs with "First," "Second," and "Third" to mark the development of three related points. Of course, any standard writing manual will contain lists of transitional expressions that are commonly used in formal writing.

These transitions should not be overused, however. Especially in a short review, it may not be necessary to use such phrases to label the development of three related points when each is described in three adjacent paragraphs. Another problem often found in short reviews is the overuse of what Bem (1995) calls "meta-comments," which are comments about the review *itself* (as opposed to

---

[4] Chen, E., Bloomberg, G. R., Fisher, E. B., & Strunk, R. C. (2003). Predictors of repeat hospitalizations in children with asthma: The role of psychosocial and socioenvironmental factors. *Health Psychology, 22,* 12–18.

comments about the literature being reviewed).[5] For instance, in Example 8.6.1, the writer restates the organization of the review (i.e., this is an example of a meta-comment) partway through the document. While there is nothing inherently wrong with making meta-comments, you should avoid frequent restatements that rehash what you have already stated.

Example 8.6.1

Example of overuse of meta-comments:

Recall that this paper deals with how question asking in children has been used to explain a variety of learning styles. Also recall that we have reviewed the research on the use of question asking in the classroom and have reached some tentative conclusions regarding its conclusions. Now, we will consider two basic types of questions that young children frequently ask, noting that….

✔ Guideline 7: Consider preparing a table that compares important characteristics of the studies reviewed.

It is sometimes useful to prepare a table that displays the main characteristics of the studies you have reviewed, especially if the research you have reviewed is of a single type. For instance, the table in Example 8.7.1 describes the important characteristics of a set of related studies. Such tables are especially helpful when there are many studies to be covered in a review. Despite the presentation of such a table, the writer of a review is still obligated to discuss in paragraph form at least the more important studies cited.

Example 8.7.1

Small portion of a hypothetical table summarizing many studies comparing phonics and whole language methods for teaching reading:

	Date	Size of Sample	Ages	Superior Method	Location
Brown (2004)	2002	120	7–9	Phonics	Texas
Cohen (2000)	1998	1,500	6–8	Phonics	California
Ebersoll (2001)	2004	800	5–6	Whole Language	Washington

✔ Guideline 8: If your topic reaches across disciplines, consider reviewing studies from each discipline separately.

Some topics naturally transcend discipline boundaries. For instance, if you were writing about diabetes management among teenage girls, you would find relevant sources in several discipline areas, including health care, nutrition, and

---

[5] Bem, D. J. (1995). Writing a review article for *Psychological Bulletin. Psychological Bulletin, 118,* 172–177.

psychology. The health care literature, for example, may deal with variations in insulin therapies (such as variations in types of insulin used or the use of pumps vs. syringes to deliver the insulin). The nutrition journals, on the other hand, may include studies on alternative methods for managing food intake in the search for more effective methods to control episodes of insulin shock. Finally, the psychological literature may offer insights into the nature of the stressors common to adolescent girls, especially with respect to how these stressors may interfere with the girls' decision-making processes concerning self-monitoring, nutrition choices, and value orientations. While these examples are hypothetical, it is easy to see how such a review might benefit from being divided into three sections, with the findings from each discipline area reviewed separately.

✔ Guideline 9:   Write a conclusion for the end of the review.

The end of your literature review should provide closure for the reader, that is, the path of the argument should end with a conclusion of some kind. How you end a literature review, however, will depend on your reasons for writing it. If the review was written to stand alone, as in the case of a term paper or a review article for publication, the conclusion needs to make clear how the material in the body of the review has supported the assertion or proposition presented in the introduction. On the other hand, a review in a thesis, dissertation, or journal article presenting original research usually leads to the research questions that will be addressed.

If your review is long and complex, you should briefly summarize the main threads of your argument, and then present your conclusion. Otherwise, you may cause your reader to pause in order to try to reconstruct the case you have made. Shorter reviews usually do not require a summary, but this judgment will depend on the complexity of the argument you have presented. You may need feedback from your faculty adviser or a friend to help you determine how much you will need to restate at the end. Example 8.9.1 presents only half of the two-paragraph summary of a very complex and comprehensive literature review. The reviewer follows this with a series of detailed recommendations (a) for future research by scholars interested in family processes and family functioning and (b) for the application of these findings in the marriage and family counseling therapeutic setting, which are not shown in the example.

Example 8.9.1[6]

Example of a summary for a complex review:

Given the growing ability of outsiders to unveil family secrets, the findings of this review may prove useful to researchers interested in the literature on controlling or withholding information in the family arena. A greater understanding of the family becomes possible through the study of secrets.

---

[6] Brown-Smith, N. (1998). Family secrets. *Journal of Family Issues, 19,* 20–42.

Whereas some scholars defined secrecy in negative terms, others compared it to the more socially accepted concept of privacy. However, a more neutral view of secrecy allows the opportunity to broaden its scope. For instance, previously offered definitions did not allow researchers the opportunity to explore secrecy in a variety of contexts as the focus was only on that which was negatively valued. (p. 39)

✓ Guideline 10: Check the flow of your argument for coherence.

One of the most difficult skills to learn in academic writing is to evaluate one's own writing for coherence. Coherence refers to how well a manuscript holds together as a unified document. It is important for you to ask yourself how well the various elements of your review connect with one another. This requires that you carefully evaluate the effectiveness of the rhetorical elements of your document that tell the reader about its structure and about the relationships among its elements. Subheadings often go a long way in identifying a manuscript's structure. Transitional expressions and other kinds of rhetorical markers also help to identify relationships among sections, as in "the next example," "in a related study," "a counter-example," and "the most recent (or relevant) study." Obviously, there are many more such examples. Remember, these kinds of rhetorical devices are useful navigational tools for your reader, especially if the details of the review are complex.

Activities for Chapter 8

1. Reread the review articles in the Supplementary Readings at the end of this book, and locate the paragraph(s), *if any*, in which the authors initially provide overviews of their reviews. Are any of the overviews particularly helpful in setting the stage for readers of the reviews? Explain.

2. Consider the subheadings in the literature reviews at the end of this book.
   - What function do the subheadings play in advancing the "argument" of the literature review?
   - To what extent do the subheadings help the reader know what will and will not be covered in the reviews?

3. In the literature reviews at the end of this book, locate three examples that illustrate the use of transitions. Were the transitions needed? Explain.

4. Locate the conclusions in the reviews at the end of this book. Which one presents the most straightforward summary of the contents of the review? Explain.

Chapter 9

Guidelines on Style, Mechanics, and Language Usage

The previous two chapters dealt with more general issues involved in writing a literature review. This chapter presents guidelines that are designed to focus on more specific issues related to style, mechanics, and language usage. These issues are important in producing a draft that is free of mechanical errors.

✔ Guideline 1: Compare your draft with your topic outline.

The topic outline you prepared after reading Chapter 6 traced the path of the argument of your literature review. Now that your first draft is completed, you need to compare what you have written with the topic outline to make sure you have properly fleshed out the path of the argument.

✔ Guideline 2: Check the structure of your review for parallelism.

The reader of a literature review, especially a complex review, needs to be able to follow the structure of the manuscript while internalizing the details of the analysis and synthesis of the individual studies you have discussed. A topic outline will typically involve parallel structural elements. For example, a discussion of weaknesses will be balanced by a discussion of strengths, arguments for a position will be balanced by arguments against, and so on. These expectations on the part of the reader stem from long-standing rhetorical traditions in academic writing. Therefore, you need to check your manuscript to make sure that your descriptions are balanced properly. This may require that you explain a particular lack of parallelism, perhaps by stating explicitly that no studies were found that contradict a specific point (see Guideline 8 in Chapter 7 if this applies to your review).

✔ Guideline 3: Avoid overusing direct quotations, especially long ones.

One of the most stubborn problems for novice academic writers in the social and behavioral sciences is the overuse of quotations. This is understandable, given the heavy emphasis placed in college writing classes on the correct use of the conventions for citing others' words. In fact, there is nothing inherently wrong about using direct quotations. However, problems arise when they are used inappropriately or indiscriminately.

A direct quotation presented out of context may not convey the full meaning of the original author's intent. When a reader struggles to understand the function of a quotation in a review, the communication of the message of the review is interrupted. Explaining the full context of a quotation can further confuse the reader with details that are not essential for the purpose of the review in hand. By contrast, paraphrasing the main ideas of an author is usually more efficient and makes it easier to avoid extraneous details. In addition, paraphrasing eliminates the potential for disruptions in the flow of a review due to the different writing styles of various authors.

Of course, direct quotations are appropriate at times. For instance, you may want to use an excerpt that was written with a particular flair or that gives an emotional kick. Or, you may want to illustrate the original author's skill in writing or lack thereof. There may be other reasons for using direct quotations. However, they should be used sparingly, and long quotations should almost always be avoided altogether. Furthermore, quotations should not stand alone, isolated conceptually from the prose that immediately surrounds them. Put another way, each quotation should be introduced by you. Example 9.3.1 illustrates an effective use of a direct quotation. Note that in this example, the writer emphasizes the poignancy of Akers' words in introducing the quotation, and then follows it up with an interpretation, thereby establishing context for the quotation.

Example 9.3.1[1]

Direct quotation (should be used sparingly):

Unfortunately, as Ronald Akers poignantly pointed out (1996, p. 11), "…in most public discourse about criminal justice policy, the underlying theoretical notions are ill-stated and vaguely understood. A policy may be adopted for political, economic, or bureaucratic reasons, then a theoretical rationale is formulated or adopted to justify the policy." As a consequence, a program may be driven by no single coherent theory but instead by an admixture of several or even conflicting theoretical positions. (p. 329)

Finally, it is seldom acceptable to begin a literature review with a quotation. Some students find it hard to resist doing this. Remember that it is usually very difficult for the reader to experience the intended impact of the quotation when it is presented before the author of the literature review has established the proper context.

---

[1] Zhang, S. X. (1998). In search of hopeful glimpses: A critique of research strategies in current boot camp evaluations. *Crime & Delinquency, 44*, 314–334.

✔ Guideline 4: Check your style manual for correct use of citations.

Make sure to check the style manual used in your field for the appropriate conventions for citing references in the text. For example, the *Publication Manual of the American Psychological Association* specifies the following guidelines for citations.

a. You may formally cite a reference in your narrative in one of several ways. At the conclusion of a statement that represents someone else's thoughts, you cite the author's last name and the year of publication, separated by a comma, set off in parentheses, as in this example: (Doe, 2003). If you use the author's name in the narrative, simply give the year of publication in parentheses immediately following the name, as in "Doe (2003) noted that...."

b. When you cite multiple authors' names in parentheses, use the ampersand (&) instead of the word "and." If the citation is in the narrative, use the word "and."

c. Use semicolons to separate multiple citations in parentheses, as in this example: (Black, 2002; Brown, 2001; Green, 2004).

d. When you cite a secondary source, be sure you have made it clear, as in this example: (Doe, as cited in Smith, 2004). Note that only Smith (2004) would be placed in the reference list.

✔ Guideline 5: Avoid using synonyms for recurring words.

The focus of a review of empirical research should be on presenting, interpreting, and synthesizing other writers' ideas and research findings as clearly and precisely as possible. This may require you to repeat words that describe routine aspects of several studies. Students who are new to academic writing sometimes approach the task as though it were a creative writing exercise. *It is not!* Literature reviews should include information about many studies (and other types of literature), all of which readers should be able to internalize quickly. Therefore, it is important to adhere to the use of conventional terms, even if they should recur. Clarity is best achieved when the writer consistently uses conventional terms throughout, especially when referring to details about a study's methodology or some other technical aspect of the research.

In general, it is best not to vary the use of labels. For example, if a study deals with two groups of participants, and the researcher has labeled them Groups 1 and 2, you should usually avoid substituting more creative phrases (e.g., "the Phoenix cohort" or "the original group of youngsters"). On the other hand, if alternative labels help clarify a study's design (e.g., when Group 1 is the control group and Group 2 the experimental group), use the substitute expressions instead, but remain consistent throughout your discussion. Example 9.5.1 illustrates how the use of synonyms and "creative" sentence construction can confuse readers. At various points, the first group is referred to as the "Phoenix cohort," as "Group I," and as the "experimental group," which is bound to cause confusion. Example 9.5.2 is an improved version in which the writer consistently uses the terms "experimental group" and "control group" to identify the two groups.

Example 9.5.1

Inconsistent use of identifying terms:

The Phoenix cohort, which was taught to correctly identify the various toy animals by name, was brought back to be studied by the researchers twice, once after six months and again at the end of the year. The other group of youngsters was asked to answer the set of questions only once, after six months, but they had been taught to label the animals by color rather than by name. The performance of Group I was superior to the performance of Group II. The superior performance of the experimental group was attributed to....

Example 9.5.2

Improved version of Example 9.5.1:

The experimental group was taught to identify toy animals by color and was retested twice at six-month intervals. The control group, which was taught to identify the toys by name, was retested only once after six months. The performance of the experimental group was superior to the performance of the control group. The superior performance of the experimental group was attributed to....

✔ Guideline 6: Spell out all acronyms when you first use them, and avoid using too many.

So many acronyms have become part of our everyday lexicon that it is easy to overlook them during the editing process. Some examples are school acronyms, such as UCLA and USC; professional acronyms, such as APA and MLA; and acronyms from our everyday lives, such as FBI, FDA, and GPA. As obvious as this guideline may seem, it is quite common to find these and other examples of acronyms that are never spelled out. Make sure to check your document carefully for acronyms and spell them out the first time you use them.

Sometimes, it is useful to refer to something by its acronym, especially if its full title is long and you need to refer to it several times. For example, the Graduate Writing Assessment Requirement (GWAR) for students in the California State University system is commonly referred to as the GWAR. In general, you should avoid using too many acronyms, especially ones that are not commonly recognized, like GWAR. In a complex literature review, using a few acronyms may be helpful, but using too many of them may be confusing.

✔ **Guideline 7:   Avoid the use of contractions; they are inappropriate in formal academic writing.**

Contractions are a natural part of language use. They are one example of the natural process of linguistic simplification that accounts for how all languages change, slowly but surely, across time. Many instructors, even some English composition instructors, tolerate the use of contractions on the assumption that their use reflects the changing standards of acceptability in modern-day American English. In spite of such attitudes, however, it is almost always *inappropriate* to use contractions in formal academic writing.

✔ **Guideline 8:   When used, coined terms should be set off in quotations.**

It is sometimes useful to coin a term to describe something in one or two words that would otherwise require a sentence or more. Coined terms frequently become part of common usage, as in the noun "lunch," which is now commonly used as a verb (Did you *lunch* with Jane yesterday?). However, coined terms should be used sparingly in formal academic writing. When you feel you should coin a term, set it off with quotation marks to indicate that its meaning cannot be found in a standard dictionary.

✔ **Guideline 9:   Avoid slang expressions, colloquialisms, and idioms.**

Remember that academic writing is *formal* writing. Therefore, slang, colloquialisms, and idioms are not appropriate in a literature review. While many slang terms such as "cool" (meaning "good") and "ain't" are becoming part of our conversational language repertoires, they should be avoided altogether in formal writing. Colloquialisms, such as "thing" and "stuff" should be replaced by appropriate noncolloquial terms (e.g., "item," "feature," and "characteristic"). Similarly, idioms, such as "to rise to the pinnacle" and "to survive the test," should be replaced by more formal expressions, such as "to become prominent" and "to succeed" or "to be successful."

✔ **Guideline 10:   Use Latin abbreviations in parenthetic material; elsewhere, use English translations.**

The Latin abbreviations shown below, with their English translations, are commonly used in formal academic writing. With the exception of et al., these abbreviations are limited to parenthetic material. For instance, the Latin abbreviation in parentheses at the end of this sentence is proper: (i.e., this is a correct example). If this was not in parentheses, you should use the English translation, that is, this is also a correct example. Also, note the punctuation that is required for each of these abbreviations. Note especially that there is no period mark after "et" in et al.

cf.	compare	e.g.,	for example	et al.	and others
etc.	and so forth	i.e.,	that is	vs.	versus, against

✓ Guideline 11: Check your draft for common writing conventions.

There are a number of additional writing conventions that all academic disciplines require. Check your draft to ensure you have applied all the following items before you give it to your instructor to read.

a. Make sure you have used complete sentences.

b. It is sometimes acceptable to write a literature review in the first person. However, you should avoid excessive use of the first person.

c. It is inappropriate to use sexist language in academic writing. For instance, it is incorrect to always use masculine or feminine pronouns (he, him, his vs. she, her, hers) to refer to a person when you are not sure of the person's gender (as in, "the teacher left her classroom...," when the teacher's gender is not known). Often, sexist language can be avoided by using the plural form ("the teachers left their classrooms..."). If you must use singular forms, alternate between masculine and feminine forms or use "he or she."

d. You should strive for clarity in your writing. Thus, you should avoid indirect sentence constructions, such as "In Smith's study, it was found...." An improved version would be, "Smith found that ...."

e. In general, numbers from zero through nine are spelled out, but numbers 10 and above are written as numbers. Two exceptions to this rule are numbers assigned to a table or figure and measurements expressed in decimals or in metrical units.

f. Always capitalize nouns followed by numerals or letters when they denote a specific place in a numbered series. For instance, this is Item f under Guideline 11 in Chapter 9. (Note that "I," "G," and "C" are capped.)

g. Always spell out a number when it is the first word or phrase in a sentence, as in, "Seventy-five participants were interviewed...." Sometimes a sentence can be rewritten so that the number is not at the beginning. For example: "Researchers interviewed 75 participants...."

✔ **Guideline 12: Write a concise and descriptive title for the review.**

The title of a literature review should identify the field of study you have investigated as well as tell the reader your point of view. However, it should also be concise and describe what you have written. In general, the title should not draw attention to itself; rather, it should help the reader to adopt a proper frame of reference with which to read your paper. The following suggestions will help you to avoid some common problems with titles.

a. **Identify the field, but do not describe it fully.** Especially with long and complex reviews, it is not advisable for you to try to describe every aspect of your argument. If you do, the result will be an excessively long and detailed title. Your title should provide your reader an easy entry into your paper. It should not force the reader to pause in order to decipher it.

b. **Consider specifying your bias, orientation, or delimitations.** If your review is written with an identifiable bias, orientation, or delimitation, it may be desirable to specify it in the title. For instance, if you are critical of some aspect of the literature, consider using a phrase such as "A Critique of..." or "A Critical Evaluation of..." as part of your title. Subtitles often can be used effectively for this purpose. For example, "The Politics of Abortion: A Review of the Qualitative Research" has a subtitle that indicates that the review is delimited to qualitative research.

c. **Avoid "cute" titles.** Avoid the use of puns, alliteration, or other literary devices that detract from the content of the title. While a title such as "Phonics vs. 'Hole' Language" may seem clever if your review is critical of the whole language approach to reading instruction, it will probably distract readers. A more descriptive title, such as "Reading as a Natural or Unnatural Outgrowth of Spoken Language," will give the reader of your review a better start in comprehending your paper.

d. **Keep it short.** Titles should be short and to the point. Professional conference organizers will often limit titles of submissions to about nine words in order to facilitate the printing of hundreds of titles in their program books. While such printing constraints are not at play with a term paper or a chapter heading, it is still advisable to try to keep your review title as simple and short as possible. A good rule of thumb is to aim for a title of about 10 words, plus or minus three.

✔ **Guideline 13: Strive for a user-friendly draft.**

You should view your first draft as a work in progress. As such, it should be formatted in a way that invites comments from your readers. Thus, it should be legible and laid out in a way that allows the reader to react to your ideas easily. The following list contains some suggestions for ensuring that your draft is user-friendly. Ask your faculty adviser to review this list, and add additional items as appropriate.

a. **Spell-check, proofread, and edit your manuscript.** New word processing programs have spell-check functions. Use the spell-check feature before asking anyone to read your paper. However, there is no substitute for editing your own manuscript carefully, especially since the spell-check function can overlook some of your mistakes (e.g., "see" and "sea" are both correctly spelled, but the spell-check function will not highlight them as errors if you mistakenly type the wrong one). Remember that your goal should be to have an error-free document that communicates the content easily and does not distract the reader with careless mechanical errors.

b. **Number all pages.** Professors sometimes write general comments in the form of a memo in addition to their notes in the margins. Unnumbered pages make such comments more difficult to write because professors cannot refer to page numbers in their memos.

c. **Double-space the draft.** Single-spaced documents make it difficult for the reader to write specific comments or suggest alternative phrasing.

d. **Use wide margins.** Narrow margins may save paper, but they restrict the amount of space available for your instructor's comments.

e. **Use a stapler or a strong binder clip to secure the draft.** Your draft is one of many papers your instructor will read. Securing the document with a stapler or a strong clip will make it easier to keep your paper together. If you use a folder or a binder to hold your draft, make sure that it opens flat. Plastic folders that do not open flat make it difficult for your professor (or editor) to write comments in the margins.

f. **Identify yourself as the author, and include a telephone number or e-mail address.** Because your draft is one of many papers your instructor will read, it is important to identify yourself as the author. Always include a cover page with your name and a telephone number or e-mail address in case your professor wants to contact you. If you are writing the literature review as a term paper, be sure to indicate the course number and title as well as the date.

g. **Make sure the draft is printed clearly.** In general, you should avoid using printers with ribbons unless you make sure the print is dark enough for it to be read comfortably. Similarly, if you submit a photocopy of your draft, make sure the copy is dark enough. Always keep a hard copy for your records! Student papers sometimes get misplaced, and hard drives on computers sometimes crash.

h. **Avoid "cute" touches.** In general, you should avoid using color text for highlighted words (use italics instead), mixing different size fonts (use a uniform font size throughout except for the title), or using clip-art or any other special touches that may distract the reader by calling attention to the physical appearance of your paper instead of its content.

✔ Guideline 14: Avoid plagiarism at all costs.

If you are uncertain about what constitutes plagiarism, consult your university's student code of conduct. It is usually part of your university's main catalog and is reprinted in several other sources readily available to students. For example, the University of Washington's Psychology Writing Center makes a handout on Plagiarism and Student Writing available on its Web site at http://depts.washington.edu/psywc/. On the main page, click the "Handouts" link, which will take you to a list of handouts in PDF format. Under the "About Plagiarism" heading, you will find a statement on academic responsibility prepared by the University's Committee on Academic Conduct (1994),[2] which discusses six types of plagiarism.

(1) Using another writer's words without proper citation;

(2) using another writer's ideas without proper citation;

(3) citing a source but reproducing the exact words of a printed source without quotation marks;

(4) borrowing the structure of another author's phrases or sentences without crediting the author from whom it came;

(5) borrowing all or part of another student's paper or using someone else's outline to write your own paper; and

(6) using a paper-writing service or having a friend write the paper for you. (p. 23)

It is easy to quarrel about whether borrowing even one or two words would constitute plagiarism or whether an "idea" is really owned by an author. However, plagiarism is easily avoided simply by making sure that you cite your sources properly. If you have any doubt about this issue with respect to your own writing, ask your instructor. This is a very serious matter.

✔ Guideline 15: Get help if you need it.

It should be obvious from the content of this chapter that the expectations for correctness and accuracy in academic writing are quite high. If you feel that you are unable to meet these demands at your current level of writing proficiency, you may need to get help. International students are often advised to hire proofreaders to help them meet their instructors' expectations. Most universities offer writing classes, either through the English department or in other disciplines. Some offer workshops for students struggling with the demands of thesis or

---

[2] Committee on Academic Conduct. (1994). *Bachelor's degree handbook*, University of Washington.

dissertation requirements, and many universities have Writing Centers that provide a variety of services for students. If you feel you need help, talk with your instructor about the services available at your university. You should not expect your instructor to edit your work for style and mechanics.

Activities for Chapter 9

1. Compare the titles of the review articles in the Supplementary Readings.
   * How well does each title serve to identify the field of the review?
   * Do the titles of the articles specify the authors' point of view in the review?

2. Now consider your own first draft of your literature review.
   * Compare your first draft with the topic outline you prepared. Do they match? If not, where did your draft vary from the outline? Does this variation affect the path of the "argument" of your review?
   * Find two or three places in your review where your discussion jumps to the next major category of your topic outline. How will the reader know that you have changed to a new category (i.e., did you use subheadings or transitions to signal the switch)?

Chapter 10

Incorporating Feedback and Refining the First Draft

At this point in the writing process, you have completed the major portion of your critical review of the literature. However, your work is not yet done. You should now undertake the important final steps in the writing process—redrafting your review.

New writers often experience frustration at this stage because they are now expected to take an impartial view of a piece of writing in which they have had a very personal role. In the earlier stages, as the writer, you were the one who was analyzing, evaluating, and synthesizing other writers' work. Now, your draft is the subject of your own and your readers' analysis and evaluation. This is not an easy task, but it is a critical *and* necessary next step in writing an *effective* literature review.

The first step in accomplishing this role reversal is to put the manuscript aside for a period of time, thereby creating some distance from the manuscript and from your role as the writer. Second, remind yourself that the writing process is an ongoing negotiation between a writer and the intended audience. This is why the role reversal is so important. You should now approach your draft from the perspective of someone who is trying to read and understand the argument that is being communicated.

The redrafting process typically involves evaluating and incorporating feedback. That feedback may come from an instructor and your peers, or it may come from your own attempts to refine and revise your own draft. If you are writing a literature review as a term paper, you should solicit feedback from your professor at key points during the writing process, either by discussing your ideas during an office visit or, if your professor is willing, by submitting a first draft for comments. If it is for a thesis or dissertation, your earliest feedback will be from your faculty adviser, although you should also consider asking fellow students and colleagues for comments. If the review is for an article intended for publication, you should seek feedback from instructors, fellow students, and colleagues.

As the writer, you should determine which comments you will incorporate and which you will discard, but the feedback you receive from these various sources will give you valuable information on how to improve the communication of your ideas to your audience. The following guidelines are designed to help you through this process.

✓ Guideline 1: The reader is always right.

This guideline is deliberately overstated to draw your attention to it because it is the most important one in the redrafting process. If an educated reader does not understand one of your points, the communication process has not worked. Therefore, you should almost always seriously consider changing the draft to make it clearer for the reader. It will usually be counterproductive to defend the draft manuscript. Instead, you should try to determine why the reader did not understand it. Did you err in your analysis? Did you provide insufficient background information? Would the addition of more explicit transitions between sections make it clearer? These questions, and others like these, should guide your discussions with your readers.

✓ Guideline 2: Expect your instructor to comment on the content.

It is important for you to obtain your instructor's feedback on the *content* of your manuscript early in the redrafting process. If your first draft contained many stylistic and mechanical errors, such as misspellings or misplaced headings, your instructor may feel compelled to focus on these matters and defer the comments on the content until the manuscript is easier to read. If this occurs, be prepared to ask your instructor for additional feedback on your paper's content. Furthermore, even if your instructor returns your draft with few marks and comments, you should not assume that silence about your paper's content means that there is no room for improvement. You should ask your instructor specific questions about your paper to generate the kind of feedback you need in order to properly revise your manuscript. Did you cover the literature adequately? Are your conclusions about the topic justified? Are there gaps in your review? How can the paper be improved? You need, and are entitled to, answers to questions such as these at this stage in the process.

✓ Guideline 3: Concentrate first on comments about your ideas.

As the previous two guidelines suggest, your first priority at this stage should be to make sure that your ideas have come across as you intended. Of course, you should note comments about stylistic matters and eventually attend to them, but your first order of business should be to ensure that you have communicated the argument you have developed. Thus, you need to carefully evaluate the feedback you receive from all your sources—your fellow students as well as your instructor—because at this stage you need to concentrate your efforts on making sure that your paper communicates your ideas effectively and correctly. (Some important matters concerning style, language use, and grammar are covered in the next chapter.)

✓ Guideline 4:   Reconcile contradictory feedback by seeking clarification.

Inevitably, you will encounter differences of opinion among those who review your draft document. For instance, it is not unusual for members of a thesis or dissertation committee to give you contradictory feedback. One member may ask that you provide additional details about a study while another member may want you to de-emphasize it. If you encounter such differences of opinion, it is your responsibility to seek further clarification from both sources and to negotiate a resolution of the controversy. First, you should make sure that the different opinions were not due to one person's failure to comprehend your argument. Second, you should discuss the matter with both individuals and arrive at a compromise solution.

✓ Guideline 5:   Reconcile comments about style with your style manual.

Make sure that you have carefully reviewed the particular style manual that is required for your specific writing task. If your earliest experience with academic writing was in an English department course, you may have been trained to use the style manual of the Modern Language Association.[1] Many university libraries advise that theses and dissertations follow the University of Chicago style manual.[2] However, the most widely used manual in the social and behavioral sciences is the style manual of the American Psychological Association.[3] If you are preparing a paper for publication, check the specific periodical or publisher for guidelines on style before submitting the paper. Finally, many academic departments and schools will have their own policies with respect to style. Regardless of which style manual pertains to your writing task, remember that you are expected to adhere to it meticulously. As you consider incorporating any feedback you receive, make sure that it conforms to the required style manual.

✓ Guideline 6:   Allow plenty of time for the feedback and redrafting process.

Students often experience frustration when they are faced with major structural or content revisions and have an imminent deadline. You can expect to have to prepare at least one major redraft of your literature review, so you should allow yourself plenty of time for it. Professional writers often go through three or

---

[1] Gibaldi, J. (1998). *MLA style manual and guide to scholarly publishing* (2nd ed.). New York: Modern Language Association of America.

[2] University of Chicago Press. (1993). *The Chicago manual of style* (14th ed.). Chicago: University of Chicago Press.

[3] American Psychological Association. (2001). *Publication manual of the American Psychological Association* (4th ed.). Washington, DC: American Psychological Association.

more drafts before they consider a document to be a final draft. While you may not have quite so many drafts, you should allow enough time to comfortably go through at least several revisions of your document.

Activities for Chapter 10

1. Ask two friends to read the draft of your literature review and comment on the content. Compare their comments.
   - On which points did your friends agree?
   - On which points did they disagree? Which of the two opinions will you follow? Why?
   - Consider the places in your review that your friends found hard to follow. Rewrite these passages, keeping in mind that you want your friends to understand your points.

2. Write five questions designed to guide your instructor or your friends in giving you feedback on the content of your review.
   - Reread your review draft, and respond to your own questions by pretending you are your instructor.
   - Revise your draft according to your own feedback.
   - Reconsider the five questions you wrote for your instructor. Which questions would you leave on your list? What questions would you add?

Chapter 11

Comprehensive Self-Editing Checklist for Refining the Final Draft

As has been emphasized frequently in this book, your final draft should be as accurate and error-free as possible, both in terms of its content as well as its mechanics and style. After you have carefully considered the feedback you received from your peers and academic advisers and after you have revised the manuscript in light of their input, you should carefully edit your manuscript a final time. The purpose for this final review is accuracy.

The following checklist is grouped according to some of the major criteria instructors use in evaluating student writing. Most of these criteria are absolutely critical when writing a thesis or dissertation. However, your instructor may relax some of them in the case of term papers written during a single semester.

You will find that most of the items on the checklist were presented in the earlier chapters as guidelines, but many additional ones have been added in an attempt to cover common problems that are sometimes overlooked by student writers. You should show this checklist to your instructors and ask that they add or eliminate items according to their own preferences.

Keep in mind that the checklist is designed to help you to refine the manuscript. Ultimately, the extent of perfection you achieve will depend on how meticulously you edit your own work.

Adherence to the Writing Process for Editing and Redrafting

_____ 1. Have you asked your instructors to review this checklist and to add or delete items according to their preferences?

_____ 2. After finishing your last draft, did you set your manuscript aside for several days before you began to revise it (i.e., did you create an appropriate *distance* from your manuscript before changing roles from "writer" to "reader")?

_____ 3. Did you ask another person to review your manuscript?

_____ 4. Have you addressed all the questions raised by your reviewers?

_____ 5. Did you reconcile all differences of opinion among your reviewers?

Importance or Significance of the Topic

_____ 6. Is your topic important, either from a theoretical or a practical perspective?

_____ 7. Does it present a fresh perspective or identify a gap in the literature (i.e., does it address a question not previously addressed)?

_____ 8. Is your topic's significance or importance demonstrated and justified?

_____ 9. Is this an appropriate topic for your field of study?

_____ 10. Is the topic timely in terms of what is being reported in the research literature?

_____ 11. Does the title of your manuscript adequately describe the subject of your review?

Organization and Other Global Considerations

_____ 12. Does your review include an introduction and a discussion and conclusions section?

_____ 13. Did you include a reference list?

_____ 14. Does the length and organization of your review follow the criteria set forth by (a) your instructor, if you are writing a term paper; (b) your committee chair, if you are writing a thesis or dissertation; or (c) the publication guidelines of the journal you have targeted, if you are writing for publication?

Effectiveness of the Introduction

_____ 15. Does your introduction describe the scope of the literature you have reviewed and why the topic is important?

_____ 16. Did you describe in your introduction the general structure of your paper?

_____ 17. Does your introduction identify the line of argumentation you have followed in your manuscript?

_____ 18. Does the introduction state what will and will not be covered, if this is appropriate?

_____ 19. Does the introduction specify your thesis statement or point of view, if this is relevant?

Currency and Relevance of the Literature Cited

_____ 20. Did you review the most current articles on the topic?

_____ 21. Are the studies you reviewed current?

_____ 22. If you have included older articles, did you have a good reason for including them?

_____ 23. Have you explained why you have described some findings as being strong?

_____ 24. Have you explained why you have described other findings as being weak?

_____ 25. Did you identify the major patterns or trends in the literature?

_____ 26. Have you identified in your manuscript the classic or landmark studies you cited?

_____ 27. Did you specify the relationship of these classic studies to subsequent studies they may have influenced?

Thoroughness and Accuracy of the Literature Reviewed

_____ 28. Is the coverage of your review adequate?

_____ 29. Have you noted and explained the gaps *in the literature*?

_____ 30. Have you described any pertinent controversies in the field?

_____ 31. If you answered yes to item 30, did you make clear which studies fall on either side of the controversy?

_____ 32. Have you checked the draft for parallelism?

_____ 33. Have you noted and explained the relationships among studies, such as which ones came first? Which ones share similarities? Which ones have differences?

_____ 34. Did you indicate the source of key terms or concepts?

_____ 35. Are there gaps *in the body of your manuscript*?

Coherence and Flow of the Path of the Argument

_____ 36. Does each study you reviewed correspond with a specific part of your topic outline?

_____ 37. Have you deleted citations to studies you decided not to include in your review because they do not relate to the path of your argument?

_____ 38. Is the path of your argument made clear throughout the manuscript?

_____ 39. Does each part of your review flow logically from the preceding part?

_____ 40. If you have used "meta-comments" (see Chapter 8, Guideline 6), are they essential?

_____ 41. If you have used subheadings, do they help to advance your argument?

_____ 42. If you have not used subheadings, would adding them help advance your argument?

_____ 43. Is your manuscript coherent, or would additional transitional devices help to clarify how it holds together?

Effectiveness of the Conclusion

_____ 44. Does your conclusion provide closure for the reader?

_____ 45. Does your conclusion make reference to the line of argumentation you specified in the introduction?

Accuracy of Citations and the Reference List

_____ 46. Have you checked your style manual's guidelines for citing references in the narrative (e.g., when to use parentheses, how to cite multiple authors, and how to cite a secondary source)?

_____ 47. Have you checked each citation in the manuscript to make sure that it appears on your reference list?

_____ 48. Have you checked all entries on the reference list to make sure that each one is cited in your manuscript?

_____ 49. Have you eliminated all entries from your reference list that are not cited in the manuscript?

_____ 50. Have you checked for accuracy and consistency between the dates in your manuscript and the dates in your reference list?

_____ 51. Have you checked for accuracy between the spelling of the authors' names in your manuscript and in your reference list?

_____ 52. Are most of the dates of the studies included in the reference list within the recent past?

Mechanics and Overall Accuracy of the Manuscript

_____ 53. Did you read and edit your manuscript carefully?

_____ 54. Did you perform a final spell-check of the entire manuscript?

_____ 55. Are your margins set appropriately?

_____ 56. Did you number all the pages?

_____ 57. Is your manuscript double-spaced?

_____ 58. Did you include your full name (and, for theses and dissertations, your telephone number or e-mail address)?

Appropriateness of Style and Language Usage

_____ 59. Have you carefully reviewed the appropriate style manual for your field?

_____ 60. Have you checked your manuscript for consistency with your style manual?

_____ 61. Are your headings formatted in accordance with the guidelines specified in the appropriate style manual?

_____ 62. If you used Latin abbreviations (i.e., e.g., etc.), are they in parentheses, and have you checked for the required punctuation?

_____ 63. If you have used long quotations, are they absolutely necessary?

_____ 64. Does each quotation contribute significantly to the review?

_____ 65. Can any of these quotations be paraphrased?

_____ 66. Did you avoid the use of synonyms for important key terms and concepts?

_____ 67. If you have coined a new term, did you set it off in quotations?

_____ 68. Have you avoided slang terms, colloquialisms, and idioms?

_____ 69. Have you avoided using contractions?

_____ 70. Have you included any annotations that are not linked to the path of the argument of your review?

_____ 71. Have you avoided using a series of annotations?

_____ 72. Have you spelled out all acronyms on first mention?

_____ 73. If you have used the first person, was it appropriate?

_____ 74. Have you avoided using sexist language?

_____ 75. If you used numbers in the narrative of your review, have you checked to see if you spelled out the numbers zero through nine?

_____ 76. If you used a noun followed by a number to denote a specific place in a sequence, did you capitalize the noun (as in Item 76 of this checklist)?

_____ 77. If you used a number to begin a sentence, did you spell it out?

Grammatical Accuracy

_____ 78. Did you check your manuscript for grammatical correctness?

_____ 79. Is every sentence of your manuscript a complete sentence?

_____ 80. Have you avoided using indirect sentence constructions (as in, "In Galvan's study, it was found….")?

_____ 81. Have you been consistent in your use of tenses (e.g., if you use the present tense in describing one study's findings, did you use this same tense throughout, unless you were commenting on the historical relationship among studies)?

_____ 82. Have you checked for the proper use of commas and other punctuation marks?

_____ 83. Have you attempted to avoid using complicated sentence structures?

_____ 84. If you have any long sentences (e.g., several lines), have you attempted to break them down into two or more sentences?

_____ 85. If you have any long paragraphs (e.g., a page or longer), have you attempted to break them down into two or more paragraphs?

Additional Editing Steps for Non-Native English Speakers and Students with Serious Writing Difficulties

_____ 86. If your proficiency in English is not at a high level, have you asked a proofreader for assistance?

_____ 87. Have you checked the entire manuscript for proper article (e.g., a, an, the) usage?

_____ 88. Have you checked the manuscript for proper use of prepositions?

_____ 89. Have you checked each sentence for proper subject–verb agreement?

_____ 90. Have you checked the manuscript for the proper use of idiomatic expressions?

Guidelines Suggested by Your Instructor

_____ 91. _____

_____ 92. _____

_____ 93. _____

_____ 94. _____

_____ 95. _____

Supplementary Readings

Sample Literature Reviews for
Discussion and Evaluation

Notes:

The Role of Physical Exercise in Alcoholism Treatment and Recovery[1]

Alcohol use disorders (AUD) are among the most common of the psychiatric disorders, affecting as much as 20% of the U.S. population (Kessler, McGonagle, & Shanyang, 1994). A number of psychological treatment approaches for AUD have been shown to be effective, including cognitive–behavioral therapies, 12-step programs, skills training, and psychopharmacological medications (W. R. Miller & Hester, 1995; Read, Kahler, & Stevenson, 2001). However, despite the success of these approaches in facilitating initial treatment gains, relapse remains a major problem, with relapse rates ranging from 60% to 90% (Brownell, Marlatt, Lichtenstein, & Wilson, 1986). In light of this, and consistent with a broadening view of substance abuse treatment that includes global lifestyle changes as part of the recovery process (Agne & Paolucci, 1982; Hodgson, 1994; Marlatt, 1985), some behavioral scientists have suggested that physical exercise may be a viable adjunct treatment approach or relapse prevention strategy for AUD (Taylor, Sallis, & Needle, 1985; Tkachuk & Martin, 1999).

Exercise Applications in AUD

To our knowledge, only two controlled studies have examined the effects of an exercise intervention on alcohol use outcomes. The first of these was conducted by Sinyor, Brown, Rostant, and Seraganian (1982). In this study, 58 men and women receiving inpatient alcohol rehabilitation treatment engaged in 6 weeks of "tailored" exercise, consisting of progressively more rigorous physical exercise including stretching, calisthenics, and walking/running. Exercise participants demonstrated better abstinence outcomes posttreatment than did nonexercising participants from two comparison groups. Significant differences between exercisers and nonexercisers continued at 3-month and 18-month follow-ups. Exercisers also experienced significant reductions in percentage of body fat and increases in maximum oxygen uptake during the course of the intervention.

The Sinyor et al. (1982) study appears to be the first and only study to have examined an exercise intervention with alcoholics in treatment. Yet, methodological shortcomings limit the extent to which conclusions may be drawn from this study. For example, participants were not randomly assigned to exercise or comparison conditions. Rather, participants in the exercise condition were compared with two small ($ns = 9$ and 12) comparison groups, one consisting of exercise participants from the exercise condition who did not fully participate and the other consisting of unmatched controls from another treatment facility. Thus, enhanced drinking outcomes experienced by exercise participants could have been a function of factors other than exercise.

A later study by T. J. Murphy et al. (1986) randomly assigned heavy-drinking college students to running, meditation, or no-treatment control conditions. Participants tracked their exercise and drinking behavior using daily self-report journals over 8 weeks. At postintervention, participants assigned to either of the intervention conditions (running or meditation) demonstrated significant decreases in quantity of alcohol consumed compared with control participants. Findings from both studies are consistent in supporting a positive relationship between physical exercise and drinking outcomes.

Despite its overall methodological rigor, the T. J. Murphy et al. (1986) study was limited by small sample size (e.g., $n = 13$ in the running condition; less than $n = 20$ in any condition), reliance on self-report measures of exercise behavior, and high dropout of participants due to dissatisfaction with their group assignment. Although limited by methodological weaknesses, these studies nonetheless suggest the potential for positive outcomes to be achieved with exercise interventions for alcohol-dependent patients.

Viability of Exercise As an Intervention: The Example of Smoking

Recent research has investigated the application of exercise interventions to the treatment of substance use disorders (see Murray, 1986; Tkachuk & Martin, 1999). The effect of exercise on nicotine dependence has received the most empirical attention. Correlational studies have shown increased fitness levels to be significantly associated with decreases in smoking behaviors (Cheraskin & Ringsdorf, 1971; Hickey, Mulcahy, Bourke, Graham, & Wilson-Davis, 1975), suggesting a potentially therapeutic effect of exercise on smoking cessation.

Further, experimental research has increasingly examined the effects of exercise on smoking outcomes (e.g., Martin et al., 1997). A number of positive effects of exercise for smoking cessation have been demonstrated, including decreased craving and reduced nicotine withdrawal (Bock et al., 1999; Pomerleau et al., 1987) and effects on initial smoking cessation and maintenance of long-term non-smoking status (Marcus et al., 1999; Marcus, Albrecht, Niaura, Abrams, & Thompson, 1991; Marcus et al., 1995). The literature on exercise and smoking is relatively modest in amount, and more studies are needed to provide stronger support for exercise as a smoking cessation intervention (see Ussher, Taylor, West, & McEwen, 2000); however, research to date suggests that exercise may be a useful component of such interventions.

In light of possible overlapping etiologies for both tobacco and alcohol use disorders (Gulliver et al., 1995; Sher, Gotham, Erickson, & Wood, 1996), the literature on exercise and smoking cessation may provide a template for understanding how exercise might be applied to AUD. More research that applies exercise interventions in the treatment of alcohol-involved patients is clearly needed.

Viability of Exercise As an Intervention: AUD

Researchers have recently been called on to demonstrate not only the efficacy of a particular treatment intervention (i.e., how well the intervention works in a controlled clinical trial) but also the treatment's effectiveness (i.e., the viability of implementing the intervention in a real-world setting). Fitness-based interventions may not only have positive effects on substance use and related outcomes but may also provide a potentially cost-effective and accessible adjunct to traditional treatment.

Increasingly, decisions about the provision of treatment for substance use disorders are based not only on clinical benefit but also on evidence of cost-effectiveness (Holder, Longabaugh, Miller, & Rubonis, 1991). Using data derived from Project MATCH, Cisler and colleagues (Cisler, Holder, Longabaugh, Stout, & Zweben, 1998) estimated that the cost of implementing three common types of outpatient alcohol treatments (cognitive–behavioral, motivational enhancement, and 12-step facilitation therapies) ranged from $281 to $585 per treatment. More intensive treatments such as residential services can be much more expensive, costing over $1,000 per treatment (French, McCollister, Cacciola, Durrell, & Stephens, 2002). Research suggests that adjunct or follow-up treatments are an important component of treatment for individuals with substance use disorders and may enhance the efficacy of an initial intervention (Humphreys & Moos, 2001; Lash, Petersen, O'Connor, & Lehmann, 2001; Miller, Ninonuevo, Hoffman, & Astrachan, 1999). Yet such continuing care potentially compounds the initial treatment cost over what is likely a longer period of time. Many forms of exercise (e.g., running, exercising to fitness videotapes, swimming) require minimal expense and, as adjunctive treatments, could represent an overall cost savings as compared with traditional aftercare treatment.

Exercise offers the additional advantages of flexibility and accessibility. As the current literature does not suggest the superiority of any particular *type* of exercise in reducing drinking or bringing about other positive consequences (e.g., Correia, Carey, & Borsari, 2000; Murphy et al., 1986; Sinyor et al., 1982), individuals may choose the mode of exercise best suited to their preferences and practical needs. Further, exercise does not require a trained clinician or an identified treatment facility. Thus, those seeking to engage in exercise can do so according to their own schedule and location, without being limited to the schedule, hours, and availability of a treatment provider. Participation in exercise is not contingent on approval from an insurance provider, and individuals engaging in physical exercise programs are not limited to a prespecified number of sessions to achieve their desired outcome.

Side effects are a major consideration in choosing a primary or adjunctive treatment for AUD. Broocks et al. (1998) found both medication and exercise to be effective treatments for anxiety disorders; however, participants in the medication group (clomipramine) reported significantly more side effects than did exercise participants. Disulfiram (Antabuse) and naltrexone are currently the only two approved medications in the United States for the treatment of alcohol dependence. Although side effects of naltrexone are less than for disulfiram, both medications have potentially dangerous side effects (Medical Economics Company, 2001; Schuckit, 1996). Although vigorous exercise has been associated with a transient but increased risk for cardiovascular complications such as myocardial infarction, the incidence of such occurrences is quite low (approximately 1 incident per 2,897,057 hr of exercise; American College of Sports Medicine [ACSM], 2000). Of course, exercise has the potential for exercise-related injuries, but with proper preventive strategies (such as appropriate warm-up and cool down procedures;

ACSM, 2000), the risk of such injuries is likely to be minimal.

Rehabilitation from AUD requires physical as well as psychological recovery. Numerous studies have documented the deleterious effects of excessive alcohol use on the cardiovascular system, including increased blood pressure (Puddey, Beilin, & Vandongen, 1987; Puddey, Beilin, Vandongen, Rouse, & Rogers, 1985), degeneration of contractile functioning (Thomas, Rozanski, Renard, & Rubin, 1994), and structural changes in the heart (Rubin & Urbano-Marquez, 1994; Thomas et al., 1994). Physical exercise has been associated with *improved* cardiovascular health in alcohol-dependent samples (Frankel & Murphy, 1974; Gary & Guthrie, 1972; J. B. Murphy, 1970; Peterson & Johnstone, 1995). Other positive health changes reported in alcoholic samples as a result of exercise include significant decreases in body fat (Sinyor et al., 1982) and weight (Frankel & Murphy, 1974) and increases in muscular strength and flexibility (Peterson & Johnstone, 1995; Tsukue & Shohoji, 1981). Thus, exercise can facilitate positive changes in both physical and psychological health among alcoholics. Further, significant fitness improvements may be possible in this population despite previous physical deconditioning or impairments (Sinyor et al., 1982).

Those interested in exercise as a part of their AUD recovery do not necessarily have to commit to an intensive fitness regimen. Although participation in physical exercise has been associated with positive changes in mental health, evidence suggests that improvement in fitness outcomes is not a necessary requirement for this to occur (Berger & Owen, 1992; Doyne et al., 1987). Moreover, many studies have found that anaerobic exercise (e.g., weight training, flexibility training) also produces positive mental health changes, such as decreased depressive (Martinsen, Hoffart, & Solberg, 1989; Palmer et al., 1995) and anxiety symptoms (Berger & Owen, 1983) and increased self-concept (Williams & Cash, 1999). These encouraging findings suggest that psychological change is possible for those with differing fitness abilities and interests and that patients may benefit psychologically even from suboptimal training levels. Thus, although a specific frequency and quantity of aerobic exercise may be necessary to achieve desired physical health benefits (USDHHS, 1996), this may not be the case for positive mental health benefits.

Finally, preliminary evidence suggests that early recovery may represent a time in which individuals are open to making a variety of changes, including physical exercise, to improve their lives and the overall context of their recovery. A recent study (Read, Brown, et al., 2001) examined attitudes toward exercise in a sample of 105 individuals in intensive outpatient treatment for alcohol and other substance use disorders. Findings revealed that exercise-based interventions may be well received by persons early in AUD recovery, as participants identified a number of benefits to engaging in regular physical exercise, and many reported interest in initiating or continuing to engage in physical exercise as part of their recovery.

Despite the viability of exercise as an intervention for the treatment of AUD, some inherent risks are posed by promoting physical exercise in this population. Specifically, although exercise at moderate intensity is safe for most individuals, health risks of more vigorous exercise have been identified, particularly among sedentary individuals (ACSM, 2000). Because alcohol misuse has been associated with numerous deleterious health consequences (Wood, Vinson, & Sher, 2001), persons with AUD may be at particular risk and should undergo careful medical screening prior to beginning an exercise regimen.

Directions for Future Research

Existing studies have offered preliminary support for exercise as a viable and promising intervention for these alcohol-involved patients. However, there clearly is a need for more empirical investigation of exercise in individuals with AUD. Studies to date have relied on very small sample sizes (e.g., T. J. Murphy et al., 1986; Palmer et al., 1995; Sinyor et al., 1982), limiting generalizability and limiting statistical power to detect treatment effects. Further, exercise studies with substance abuse populations have rarely consisted of controlled trials (see Folkins & Sime, 1981; Taylor et al., 1985; Tkachuk & Martin, 1999). Instead, studies have relied on convenience samples (e.g., persons already involved in treatment with an exercise facility available), in which participants are not randomized to condition (e.g., Palmer et al., 1988; Tsukue & Shohoji, 1981; Sinyor et al., 1982). Conclusions regarding the effects of exercise on the treatment of AUD must await the conduct of carefully controlled, randomized clinical trials.

Review B

Individual Differences in Student Cheating[1]

There can be little doubt that cheating occurs among college students. There is a long history of studies on the frequency of cheating in the United States (see Davis, Grover, Becker, & McGregor, 1992, for a review), and this research has recently been extended into the United Kingdom (Franklyn-Stokes & Newstead, 1995). No precise figures can be given as to incidence because this depends on how cheating is defined and how it is measured. However, the American research has repeatedly shown that more than half of university students indulge in some form of cheating behavior during their undergraduate years, and the British studies suggest that the figure is not markedly different in the United Kingdom. Although such figures are surprising and perhaps disturbing, from a psychological perspective the more interesting questions surround the factors that influence cheating behavior and the reasons why some students cheat more than others.

The research literature on cheating has tended to be largely descriptive, so that we now know much about the incidence and correlates of cheating and much less about the reasons for the observed differences. A possible conceptual framework can be provided by considering two factors that seem inherently likely to be implicated in explaining cheating behavior: motivation and morality. The contribution of each of these will be considered in turn.

With respect to motivation, there is evidence that those with high achievement motivation are more likely to cheat than those with lower levels. Type A behavior (Friedman & Rosenman, 1959), which involves high striving for achievement, has been found to correlate positively with both observed and reported cheating (Perry, Kane, Bernesser, & Spicker, 1990; Weiss, Gilbert, Giordano, & Davis, 1993). However, the full picture is almost certainly more complicated than this because it seems likely that only some forms of achievement motivation might lead to cheating. Dweck (1986) has drawn the distinction between students with performance goals (those who wish simply to achieve good grades in their courses) and students with learning goals (those who wish to learn from their studies). Related, though not identical, distinctions have been made by Ames (1984) between ability and mastery goals and by Nicholls (1984) between ego involvement and task involvement. Individuals with learning goals are more likely to persist in challenging tasks and may even seek them out, and it is reasonable to suggest that such students will be less likely to resort to cheating as a way of coping with a challenging situation. There is little direct evidence on this issue, though Weiss et al. (1993) found that those who studied to learn (as measured by Eison's [1981] scale) rather than to obtain a good grade were less likely to cheat.

Turning now to morality, once again the direct evidence is sparse, but there is an indication that moral development is related to cheating. It has been found that scores on moral reasoning tests correlate negatively with the occurrence of cheating (Grimm, Kohlberg, & White, 1968; Malinowski & Smith, 1985). Note, however, that cheating in these studies involved cheating on experimental tasks, not on assessments. Other research has indicated that students who cheat in the classroom tend to "neutralize" (rationalize) their behavior, blaming it on the situation rather than on themselves (e.g., Haines, Diekhoff, LaBeff, & Clark, 1986). Neutralization involves denial of responsibility, condemnation of condemners, and appeal to higher authorities; all these are ways of protecting the individual from blame and, hence, from moral disapproval. Neutralization, however, is likely to be a consequence rather than a cause of cheating.

While the literature relating cheating to both motivation and morality is not voluminous, these two concepts provide a useful perspective from which to view the existing research on cheating. Most of this research is descriptive and focuses on group differences in the incidence of cheating. These differences, which have included dimensions such as gender, age, academic achievement, and discipline studied, are reviewed and, where appropriate, related to the concepts of motivation and morality.

Gender

There is considerable evidence in the literature that females report less cheating than males. This was found to be consistently the case by Davis et al. (1992) in their survey of more than 6,000 students and has also been reported by many other researchers, including Baird (1980) and Calabrese and Cochran (1990). There are, however, a number of exceptions to this finding. Haines et al. (1986) and Houston (1983) found no differences between the sexes. Jacobson, Berger, and Millham (1970) even found that females cheated significantly more often than males.

Gender differences in motivation may help explain these findings since it has been found that female university students tend to be more intrinsically motivated than male students (Vallerand et al., 1992). Intrinsically motivated students are studying for the pleasure and satisfaction of doing so and, hence, seem unlikely to cheat. Gender differences might also be related to differences in moral reasoning, though the evidence that females have a better developed sense of moral responsibility is controversial (see, for example,

Thoma, 1986). There is some evidence that females admit to as much cheating as males when this is of an altruistic nature, that is, is done to help another student (Calabrese & Cochran, 1990).

Age

Previous research has suggested that university students are less likely to cheat than those in high school (Davis et al., 1992). Some studies have found that students in the later years of their degree course are less likely to cheat than those in their early years (e.g., Bowers, 1964; Baird, 1980), though other studies have found little difference in relation to year of study (Stern & Havlicek, 1986). These differences between students of differing experience may be attributable to the fact that the more experienced students were slightly older; alternatively, they may be related to the different cultures and opportunities present in the different years of study, or to the fact that some of the weaker students, who may be more likely to cheat, have been weeded out during the early years of their course.

There is relatively little research that has looked directly at the effects of age, although this is a dimension that is becoming increasingly important in higher education as the proportion of mature and nontraditional students increases. Haines et al. (1986) found that there was a negative correlation between age of student and reported incidence of cheating; indeed, this variable was the most powerful of the many predictors of cheating that they studied in their research. Franklyn-Stokes and Newstead (1995) found in their first study that students aged 25 years or older were perceived by other students and lecturers to cheat less often than those aged either 21–24 or 18–20 years. Their second study found that both the older age group and the youngest students reported cheating less than the 21–24 year olds. This is clearly an area in which further data are required.

Motivational differences seem a plausible candidate for explaining the effects of age. There is considerable evidence that older students may be studying for more intrinsic, personal rewards than those who go straight to university from school (see Richardson, 1994, for a recent review). Explanations of age differences in terms of moral development cannot be ruled out, because there is considerable evidence for age-related development in moral reasoning, even over the short period of a degree course (Murk & Adelman, 1992; Rest & Thoma, 1985), though this may be due to the influences of education rather than age itself.

Academic Achievement

In general, it seems that more successful students are less likely to cheat. This conclusion emerges from studies that have correlated grade point average (GPA) with observed and reported incidence of cheating. Hetherington and Feldman (1964) found that student cheating in experimentally contrived situations was higher for students with low GPAs. Similarly, Bowers (1964) and Haines et al. (1986) found that GPA correlated negatively with the extent to which students reported cheating.

The achievement of high grades is, not surprisingly, related to motivation (see, for example, Pintrich & Garcia, 1991). However, it is possible that high achievers also have a better developed sense of moral responsibility and, hence, explanations in terms of both motivation and morality are possible.

Discipline Studied

A wide variety of disciplines has been studied in previous research, but it is not easy to compare such studies because they have typically used tailor-made questionnaires; therefore, direct comparisons of the frequencies of cheating are invalid. Relatively few studies have systematically compared the incidence of cheating in different disciplines. The most important study to date of interdisciplinary differences was carried out some years ago in the United States by Bowers (1964). In a national survey involving over 5,000 students in 11 different majors, he found that certain disciplines were associated with more cheating than others: Business and engineering were associated with the highest rates of cheating; education, social science, and science were in the middle; and arts and humanities had the lowest rates. It is not easy to relate these differences to either motivation or to morality. It is possible that business and engineering students tend to have performance goals whereas arts and humanities students have learning goals, but there is little direct evidence on this.

It is clear from the existing research that there are many issues requiring further clarification and elaboration. In the present research, we investigated differences in cheating as a function of gender, age, academic achievement, and discipline studied. In addition, we used a measure of the extent to which students adopted high academic standards and asked students to indicate their reasons for studying for a degree; both of these were intended to obtain insights into students' motivation.

The present research involved the use of a questionnaire designed to elicit self-reported frequency of 21 different cheating behaviors. In addition to indicating whether they had indulged in cheating, respondents were also asked to give their reasons for cheating or not cheating. Reasons for not cheating seem not to have been studied before, despite their potential theoretical and practical implications. There are, however, a number of studies that have investigated reasons for cheating and that provide indications as to what to expect. The received wisdom is that the major factors are time pressure and the competition to get good grades (e.g., Barnett & Dalton, 1981). Reasons for cheating are of particular interest because of the potential light they can shed on theories of cheating behavior: They provide information both on students' motivation and on their morality.

We designed Study 1 to investigate the incidence of a number of different cheating behaviors. This enabled us to relate this incidence to gender, age, academic achievement, academic standards, and discipline studied. By examining the reasons given for cheating and not cheating, we hoped to shed some light on the underlying causes of cheating and to relate these to current theories of motivation and moral development.

Notes:

Review C

Knowledge, Interest, and Narrative Writing[1]

In 1932, Hemingway wrote that "A good writer should know as near everything as possible" (p. 191). In the past decade, psychologists and educators have rediscovered that to know more is to write better (e.g., DeGroff, 1987; Kellogg, 1987; Langer, 1984; McCutchen, 1986; Voss, Vesonder, & Spilich, 1980). More recently, psychologists also have considered the role that interest plays in writing (e.g., Hidi & Anderson, 1992; Hidi & McLaren, 1991), although very few empirical investigations have been conducted in the area (Hidi & McLaren, 1990).

Several questions remain unanswered about the roles that knowledge and interest play in effective writing. For example, do writers' knowledge of and interest in a topic explain a significant proportion of variance in writing measures beyond that explained by students' knowledge of discourse structure? Does interest explain a significant amount of variance beyond that explained by topic knowledge? Furthermore, do knowledge and interest interact in their effects on writing? Finally, do knowledge and interest interact with gender and grade level in influencing writing? Such questions led us to investigate narrative writing.

Specifically, we examined (a) whether discourse knowledge, topic knowledge, and individual interest interact in their relationship with writing and (b) whether grade level and gender interact with topic knowledge and interest. In addition, we investigated whether topic knowledge and individual interest are related to the interestingness of writers' narrative texts. Finally, we sought empirical evidence that topic knowledge and individual interest actually measure different constructs. We begin by describing briefly the Flower and Hayes (1981) writing model, which provided the theoretical foundation for our study.

Flower and Hayes (1981) Model

Flower and Hayes (1981) proposed a model of writing processes that they derived from protocol analyses of writers as the writers composed aloud. The model has three main components: the task environment, the writer's long-term memory, and the writing processes. Elements in the task environment include the writing topic, the intended audience, motivating factors, and elements of text already produced (e.g., notes, outlines, or drafts) that provide external storage of ideas. The long-term memory component includes knowledge of the topic, audience, and types of writing plans (expository, narrative, etc.). Together, the task environment and the long-term memory influence the interactive and iterative writing processes of planning, translating, and reviewing.

Planning involves three subprocesses: generating, organizing, and goal setting. Writers generate ideas by accessing relevant information about the writing topic from long-term memory and from the task environment. Writers organize ideas by imposing a meaningful structure that fits well with readers' expectations. In goal setting, writers plan how to convey their ideas in a meaningful way to the intended audience. In translating, writers transform ideas into written text, which requires knowledge of vocabulary and of rules of standard written language. Reviewing is a continual process that involves the writer's

---

evaluation and revision of text according to internal standards and perceived audience expectations.

In this study, we limited our investigation to indicants of the planning and translating processes. Writers thus wrote only one draft of a narrative passage without having the opportunity to revise. We expected that, along with interest, two elements of long-term memory would be related to indicants of writing processes: discourse knowledge and topic knowledge.

Discourse Knowledge

Discourse knowledge concerns what one knows about how to write. More specifically, discourse knowledge "consists of schemata for various discourse forms, procedures, and strategies involved in instantiation of those schemata, and local sentence–generation procedures (including grammatical knowledge)" (McCutchen, 1986, p. 432). Such knowledge is important to writers for writing grammatically correct prose, for generating sentences that are cohesively linked, and for writing coherently. Older students presumably have more and better organized knowledge about text structure (McCutchen, 1986). In fact, writers become competent with discourse knowledge rather late in their development of literacy (Chomsky, 1965).

Discourse knowledge is important for rapid processing of verbal information. For example, Hunt and colleagues (Hunt, 1978; Hunt, Frost, & Lunneborg, 1973; Hunt, Lunneborg, & Lewis, 1975) compared high- and low-discourse knowledge college students on tasks requiring encoding, attending, rehearsing, chunking, searching long-term memory, and holding and manipulating information in long-term memory. Students with high discourse knowledge processed information more accurately and rapidly than did low-discourse knowledge students. Benton and colleagues (Benton & Kiewra, 1986; Benton, Kraft, Glover, & Plake, 1984) found similar results on tasks requiring writers to unscramble scrambled letters, words, sentences, and paragraphs. In both high school and undergraduate samples, skilled writers performed these tasks faster and more accurately than did

less skilled writers. In addition, college students' performance on the tasks was positively related to their discourse knowledge.

These findings support Kellogg's (1987) view that the relationship between discourse knowledge and writing ability may have the most to do with the translating process. Translating requires transforming ideas (semantics) into written symbols that satisfy the constraints of standard rules of the language (e.g., syntax). Discourse knowledge makes writing (i.e., translating) automatic. Writers who have easier access to knowledge of discourse (e.g., grammar, punctuation, sentence structure, and text structure) translate their ideas more rapidly and accurately and, consequently, they produce more syntactically correct prose. Therefore, measures of discourse knowledge should be correlated with indicants of the translating process.

Topic Knowledge

How much writers know about a topic influences how well they write (e.g., DeGroff, 1987; Kellogg, 1987; Langer, 1984; McCutchen, 1986; Voss et al., 1980). Langer (1984) believes this is the case because:

> Intuition and experience suggest that when students write to a topic about which they have a great deal of well-integrated knowledge, their writing is more likely to be well organized and fluent; conversely, when students know little about a topic, their writing is more likely to fail. (Langer, 1984, p. 28)

McCutchen (1986) and Voss et al. (1980) examined how topic knowledge influences narrative writing with respect to descriptions of setting and actions. McCutchen (1986) and Voss et al. (1980) argued that a person with a great deal of topic knowledge would, in addition to describing the setting of a story, generate a meaningful sequence of actions and provide detail. However, someone with little knowledge of the topic would most likely be able to describe the setting but be unable to generate a sequence of actions that is both meaningful and detailed. In fact, Voss et al. (1980) found that undergraduates who had more knowledge about baseball generated a greater proportion of baseball game-related actions than did those with less baseball knowledge. Conversely, undergraduates with less baseball knowledge wrote stories that contained a greater proportion of topic-irrelevant information. Similarly, McCutchen (1986) found that elementary and middle school students who had a great deal of football knowledge wrote expository and narrative texts that contained a greater proportion of game-related actions than did the texts of football novices. In addition, high-football-knowledge students wrote more coherent and lengthier texts than did low-football-knowledge students. DeGroff (1987) found similar results with fourth-grade students who wrote on the topic of baseball.

Topic knowledge can enhance low-ability students' performance on topic-related tasks (e.g., Recht & Leslie, 1988; Schneider, Körkel, and Weinert, 1989; Walker, 1987). For example, Walker (1987) compared the recall performance of adults with high and low aptitudes (as defined by the U. S. Army aptitude test of general or technical ability) who were also identified as either baseball experts or baseball novices. Adults with low aptitudes who were baseball experts recalled more information from a baseball passage than did the adults with high aptitudes who were baseball novices. Similarly, Recht and Leslie (1988) and Schneider et al. (1989) found that children who had greater knowledge about a topic recalled more information from a passage about that topic than did children who had less knowledge. However, Recht and Leslie (1988) and Schneider et al. (1989) found neither a main effect for aptitude nor an interaction of Aptitude × Knowledge on children's text recall and comprehension of a baseball passage. These studies suggest that differences in topic knowledge may be more important than differences in aptitude and that individuals with low aptitudes may be able to perform effectively in a domain for which they have a great deal of knowledge (Schneider et al., 1989).

Differences in topic knowledge can also reverse expected age-related differences in cognitive performance (Schneider et al., 1989). Perhaps the best known study is that by Chi (1978), who compared child chess experts with adult chess novices. Chi found that al-though children performed worse on traditional memory-span tasks, the children outperformed the adults on reproduction of chess positions that conformed to the rules of chess. Similarly, Körkel (1987) found that third-grade soccer experts recalled more text units from a soccer passage than did both fifth-grade and seventh-grade soccer novices. Together, these studies indicate that topic knowledge can enable a child expert to perform like an older expert and even better than an older novice.

Why is topic knowledge so important for the writing process? In proposing his work-load hypothesis, Kellogg (1987) stated that "the more an individual knows about a topic, the less effortful it might be to retrieve and use the relevant knowledge in preparing a written document" (p. 258). The person with high knowledge has more information in memory on which to draw and takes less time than the person with low knowledge to retrieve it. For the person with high knowledge, the ideas come so rapidly that writing becomes automatic, to the point where the pen or keyboard can hardly keep up with the generating process. Consequently, the planning process is highly automated. The writer with high knowledge has more workload space to devote to setting goals and organizing ideas. Therefore, we expected the amount of topic knowledge to be related to indicants of the generating and organizing subprocesses of planning.

Interest

Educational psychologists have long asserted that interest directs attention and enhances learning (Dewey, 1913; James, 1890; Thorndike, 1935). Psychologists have recently begun to consider the role that interest plays in writing (e.g., Hidi, 1990; Hidi & Anderson, 1992; Hidi & McLaren, 1991). Some have suggested that interest influences students' writing because it combines what students know about a topic with what they value (Hidi & McLaren, 1991; Renninger, 1992). Therefore, some authors recommend that teachers have young children select their own writing topics (Gradwohl & Schumacher, 1989; Graves, 1975).

Most researchers believe that interest emerges from an individual's interaction with his or her environment (Krapp, Hidi, & Renninger, 1992). There are two distinct types of interest: (a) *individual* interest, which emerges from one's history of interaction with an object or a stimulus and (b) *situational* interest, which pertains to the specific characteristics of an event or object that capture one's interest (Hidi, 1990). Whereas individual interest is considered more of a psychological trait, situational interest is, by definition, more state specific. Our intent in the present study was to investigate the relationship between narrative writing and individual interest. Individual interest is thought to increase attention, concentration, effort, willingness to learn, and acquisition of knowledge (Renninger, 1992). On average, individual interest has been found to correlate about .30 with measures of academic achievement. Correlations tend to be stronger among male students than among female students and among older than among younger students (Schiefele, Krapp, & Winteler, 1992).

In their review of the literature, Hidi and McLaren (1990) did not find any empirical investigations of how individual interest is related to writing performance. In a follow-up study, Hidi and McLaren (1991) found that fourth and sixth graders did not write longer or qualitatively better expositions on topics that the students identified as being interesting than they did on those they identified as being uninteresting. Hidi and McLaren (1991) also found that although students are motivated to write on topics they find interesting, lack of topic knowledge may actually hinder their writing performance. On the other hand, students' writing may be enhanced if they have high knowledge about topics that they find relatively uninteresting.

On the basis of these findings, we expected that an interaction might be observed between topic knowledge and interest in terms of effects on indicants of planning (i.e., generating and organizing ideas) processes. Specifically, we hypothesized that high knowledge and low interest would be associated with lengthier and better organized writing than would low knowledge and low interest.

In addition, high knowledge and high interest should have stronger effects than low knowledge and high interest.

Previous findings pertaining to gender and grade level differences (Schiefele et al., 1992) led us to predict that these variables might also interact with interest in their relationship to planning. In the present study, we chose the writing topic of baseball. We therefore expected male students would know more about the writing topic. Consequently, we hypothesized that male students would outperform female students at low interest levels but that female students would perform comparably to male students at high interest levels. Furthermore, whereas older writers should outperform younger writers at low interest levels, younger writers should perform comparably to older writers at high interest levels.

Purpose and Predictions

Our purpose in the present study was to investigate whether discourse knowledge, topic knowledge, and individual interest are related to different measures of narrative writing performance. We were further interested in whether topic knowledge and interest interact with discourse knowledge, gender, or grade level in their relationships with writing. Our predictions were that (a) discourse knowledge should be related to indicants of the translating process; (b) topic knowledge should be related to indicants of the planning process (i.e., generating and organizing); (c) whereas male students with low interest should write lengthier and better organized stories than female students with low interest, female students with high interest should perform comparably to male students with high interest; (d) older students should be more successful than younger students at translating ideas into correct syntactic structure; (e) a developmental reversal may be observed on indicants of the planning process for younger students with high knowledge versus older students with low knowledge; and (f) whereas older writers with low interest should outperform younger writers with low interest, high interest should enable younger writers to perform comparably to older writers.

Review D

Perfectionism and Ethnicity: Implications for Depressive Symptoms and Self-Reported Academic Achievement[1]

Attempts to further understand perfectionism have resulted in increased attention to this construct in the psychological literature over the past few decades. A large portion of that attention has focused on defining the construct. High personal standards is one characteristic of perfectionism that is consistently mentioned in the literature. Indeed, perfectionists have been described as harboring excessive personal standards both in the historical conceptual literature (Adler, 1956; Horney, 1950) and in the more recent empirical literature (Slaney & Ashby, 1996; Slaney, Chadha, Mobley, & Kennedy, 2000; Slaney, Rice, Mobley, Trippi, & Ashby, 2001), though the psychological effects of high standards have not always been detrimental (Dunkley, Blankstein, Halsall, Williams, & Winkworth, 2000; Rice & Mirzadeh, 2000; Slaney et al., 2001). Adler (1956) posited that striving for high personal standards of perfection can be a normal aspect of human growth and development.

Dimensions of Perfectionism

Despite the normality of striving to be perfect, the pervasive perception in the literature is that perfectionism is pathological (Pacht, 1984). Some researchers have extended the view of perfectionism as a multidimensional and generally deleterious construct. Hewitt and Flett (1991) described three dimensions of perfectionism and operationalized them as subscales in their Multidimensional Perfectionism Scale: self-oriented perfectionism, other-oriented perfectionism, and socially prescribed perfectionism. Self-oriented perfectionists are critical of themselves and have difficulty accepting their flaws. They tend to set high, unrealistic personal standards with which they evaluate themselves. Other-oriented perfectionists have unrealistic standards for their significant others, whereas socially prescribed perfectionists believe that other people hold high, unrealistic expectations of them, including expecting them to be perfect. They feel as though these expectations are impossible to meet.

Frost, Marten, Lahart, and Rosenblate (1990) offered a different multidimensional perspective of perfectionism. They identified six dimensions of perfectionism and also developed a Multidimensional Perfectionism Scale to tap the dimensions of high personal standards, concerns about meeting parental expectations, doubts about one's actions, preference for organization and order, excessive concern about making mistakes, and parental criticism. According to Frost et al. (1990), perfectionists are often excessively self-critical as well. Many researchers have found associations between perfectionism and a number of problems, including anxiety (Johnson & Slaney, 1996), depression (Hewitt

& Dyck, 1986; Hewitt & Flett, 1990), suicidal ideation (Hewitt, Flett, & Turnbull-Donovan, 1992), procrastination (Ferrari, 1992; Flett, Blankenstein, Hewitt, & Koledin, 1992), low self-esteem (Preusser, Rice, & Ashby, 1994), and poor adjustment (Chang, 2000; Chang & Rand, 2000).

Although several studies have examined perfectionism in a number of areas, few have focused specifically on racial or ethnic differences in perfectionism. Some exceptions include a study by Chang (1998), who compared Asian American and Caucasian American college students, and Nilsson, Paul, Lupini, and Tatem (1999), who explored differences in characteristics of perfectionism between Caucasian and African American students. The following sections provide a brief review of the perfectionism literature on Asian Americans and African Americans. Included in this review are the limited studies that explore differences in the characteristics of perfectionism between Asian Americans and Caucasian Americans and between African Americans and Caucasian Americans. The literature demonstrates a need to extend current conceptualizations of perfectionism to include a better understanding of potential differences and similarities in the characteristics of perfectionism among these three ethnic groups, with an emphasis on Asian American and African American students.

Asian Americans

Despite the growing research on multiple dimensions of perfectionism, surprisingly few studies have examined potential racial/ethnic differences in this construct. In a comprehensive review of the literature on stereotypes of Asian American students, Yee (1992) suggested that many Asian Americans could be characterized as possessing excessive perfectionistic behaviors. In fact, characteristics of perfectionism emerged for Asian Americans in Peng and Wright's (1994) analysis of data from about 25,000 students in the National Education Longitudinal Study. Specifically, compared with other racial/ethnic groups, Asian Americans reported extreme concerns about meeting high parental expectations, one of the characteristics of perfectionism accord-

ing to Frost et al.'s (1990) Multidimensional Perfectionism Scale. In their critical consideration of the academic achievements of Asian Americans, Sue and Okazaki (1990) offered cultural and social perspectives to explain achievement patterns. Among other points, they indicated that certain family values, such as demands and expectations for achievement and induction of guilt, account for potential cultural differences in achievement. For example, Asian American college students may feel pressured to meet parental expectations for success and may experience parental criticism if they do not meet those expectations. This could lead many Asian American college students to strive for perfection. As a result of this cultural view, there may be specific differences in the characteristics of perfectionism between Asian Americans and other racial/ethnic groups. However, based on this view, it is unclear whether other characteristics of perfectionism, in addition to parental expectations and parental criticism, may differ by ethnicity.

Chang (1998) used Frost et al.'s (1990) conceptualization and measurement of perfectionism and found that Asian American university students reported more doubts about their actions, concerns about making mistakes, and greater parental expectations, and they perceived more criticism from parents than Caucasian American students. It is interesting to note that he also found that the two groups did not differ significantly in personal standards and organization. Chang also found that Asian Americans reported more hopelessness and higher suicidal risk potential, such as suicidal ideation and negative self-evaluation, although they were less likely to actually attempt suicide when compared with Caucasian Americans.

African Americans

Nilsson et al. (1999) compared African American and Caucasian college students on both Multidimensional Perfectionism Scales (Frost et al., 1990; Hewitt & Flett, 1991). They found that African American students reported significantly higher scores on the Parental Expectations and Other-Oriented Perfectionism subscales and lower scores on

Concern Over Mistakes and Parental Criticism subscales, when compared with the Caucasian students. Although this was an important contribution to the literature on measuring perfectionism among racial/ethnic groups, the study did not examine possible racial differences in the way in which perfectionism relates to adjustment indicators.

Two studies have found racial differences on the Perfectionism subscale of the Eating Disorder Inventory (EDI; Garner & Olmstead, 1984; Garner, Olmstead, & Polivy, 1983). The EDI Perfectionism subscale is a unidimensional measure of problematic perfectionism, with items representing very high standards and goals. Striegel-Moore et al. (2000) reported results from a large, longitudinal growth and health study of adolescent girls. Between the ages of 11 and 14 years, African American girls reported significantly higher Perfectionism subscale scores than did Caucasian girls. Likewise, Wassenaar, le Grange, Winship, and Lachenicht (2000) examined EDI differences among South African Black, White, and Asian students (average age was 22 years) and found that Black women obtained the highest scores on the Perfectionism subscale.

Hines and Boyd-Franklin (1996) offered competing conceptual perspectives regarding parental expectations and their influence on work and educational values of African Americans. On one hand, they suggested that African American parents would expect their children to do better than they did, but "because African Americans place great value on character and generally believe in the basic worth of every individual regardless of his or her success, children who earn an honest living and are self-supporting may win as much parental approval as those who are professionals" (p. 76). On the other hand, African American children of middle-class parents "who often enter the middle class without financial assets and struggle to retain a tenuous hold on their status are likely to demand high achievement from their children" (p. 76). It would appear as though concern for the future of their children, possibly in light of racism

and oppression, might contribute to high parental demands and expectations. On the basis of this perspective, one could argue that, as a result of racism and oppression experienced by their parents, African American children may feel great pressure to succeed. Both views are possibly supported by the studies using the EDI and Multidimensional Perfectionism Scale summarized earlier. It is unclear, however, due to the lack of research, whether African Americans would experience greater depression or other problems as a result of perfectionism. This apparent gap in the literature is an important area of exploration and one of the purposes of this study.

In sum, although the conceptual literature alludes to, and existing studies support, specific differences that exist in characteristics of perfectionism among Asian Americans, African Americans, and Caucasian Americans, there is a paucity of empirical literature that addresses these differences, and even fewer studies examine differences between all three ethnic groups. As a result, we lack a comprehensive perspective of perfectionism that takes into account one's ethnicity. Specifically, we do not have a clear sense of how individuals from different ethnic backgrounds experience perfectionism and how those experiences may relate to depressive symptoms and academic achievement. Consequently, additional research is needed to examine similarities and differences that exist between various ethnic groups with regard to their scores on measures of perfectionism and the different ways in which perfectionism might relate to indicators of adjustment and achievement to provide a more inclusive and comprehensive understanding of this complex construct. To that end, we attempted to replicate and extend the current literature by proposing the following research questions: Are there differences in perfectionism scores between different ethnic groups? Are the associations between the scores on perfectionism and measures of emotional adjustment and academic achievement different for different ethnic groups?

Notes:

Appendix A

A Closer Look at Locating Literature Electronically[*]

In this topic, we will consider how to use electronic databases (i.e., databases accessible via computers) to locate articles in academic journals. Note that journal articles are the major source of original reports of empirical research as well as the primary source of information on established and emerging theories.

Three of the major databases in the social and behavioral sciences are (1) *Sociofile*, which contains *Sociological Abstracts* and *Social Planning/Policy & Development Abstracts*, covering journal articles published in more than 1,600 journals; (2) *PsycINFO*, which contains *Psychological Abstracts*, with abstracts to journal articles worldwide since 1974; and (3) *ERIC*, which contains abstracts to articles in education found in more than 600 journals from 1966 to date.[1] While the following examples illustrate the use of the *ERIC* database, the principles for searching all three databases are quite similar, except where noted below.

The best access point for the *ERIC* database is at www.AskEric.org. Unlike most other databases, access is free of charge to any user, and you can access it from any computer connected to the Internet without restrictions such as passwords. (Other electronic databases are usually free of charge to students through their college libraries, which pay license fees that permit students and professors to use them without additional charge.)

The first step in searching a database is to examine its thesaurus. At AskEric.org, click on *Eric* Search and then click on "Search *ERIC* Database" and then click on "*ERIC* Thesaurus." Click on the "Browse" button if you want to scan all the "keywords" in the database. You can also enter any term to find out if it is used by *ERIC* in classifying journal articles in the database.

The Thesaurus can help you refine your topic. For example, if you enter "Drinking" in a search of the Thesaurus, the results will give you a brief definition called a "scope note" that indicates that the term "drinking" is defined as "consumption of alcoholic beverages." It also indicates that a "narrower term" is "alcohol abuse." If you look up "alcohol abuse," you will learn that it is defined as "excessive or otherwise inappropriate ingestion of alcoholic beverages." In addition, you will learn that "alcoholism" is a "narrower term" than "alcohol abuse," while a "broader term" is "substance abuse." Related terms such as "alcohol education," "driving while intoxicated," and "fetal alcohol syndrome" are also given. With this information from the Thesaurus, you can determine which of the *ERIC* terms will be most appropriate for your literature search.

The terms found in the *ERIC* Thesaurus are known as "keywords" (formerly known as "descriptors"). In an *ERIC* search for articles with the keyword *Alcohol Abuse* (with the box to limit the results to journal articles checked), references for 957 articles will be located (as of the time of this writing).

Frequently, researchers want to narrow their database searches in order to make them more precise. An important instruction for doing this is *AND*. For example, if we use the instruction to locate articles with "*alcohol abuse AND treatment*," *ERIC* will identify only 122 articles that deal with *both* alcohol abuse *and* its treatment.

We can also make our search more precise by using *NOT*. Using the instruction "*alcohol abuse NOT college*" will identify all articles relating to alcohol abuse but exclude any that relate to alcohol abuse at the college level.

You can conduct a search for all articles containing either (or both) of two keywords by using *OR*. For example, the instruction to find "dyslexia" *OR* "learning disabilities" will locate all articles with either one of these descriptors. Thus, using *OR* broadens a search.[2]

---

[1] The emphasis in this topic is on journal articles. Note that *PsycLIT* also abstracts books, *Sociofile* also abstracts dissertations, and *ERIC* also abstracts unpublished documents, such as convention papers, which are available on microfiche.

---

[2] The terms *AND*, *NOT*, and *OR* are known as "logical operators."

A unique feature of AskEric is that it permits users to submit written questions, and employees of *ERIC* will search the literature for you (at no charge) to locate literature that relates to your question. This can be very helpful if you are having difficulty locating literature on your specific research topic.

Unlike *ERIC*, *PsycINFO* allows you to search by author. This can be helpful if you know the name of an important researcher (or theorist) in your research area and want to identify additional publications by him or her. In addition, *PsycINFO* permits a search of keywords in only the titles of publications. For instance, a search for "alcohol abuse" in any field yields an unmanageable 4,798 publications (at the time of this writing). Restricting the search to articles containing the term in their titles yields only 173 articles. These are the 173 of the 4,798 that are most likely to deal directly with alcohol abuse (as opposed to publications in which it is dealt with as a side issue) because the authors mentioned alcohol abuse in the titles of their articles.

Other important electronic databases for locating journal articles are described in Appendix C. Whichever ones you use, you will save time in the long run and conduct more useful searches if you read carefully the instructions for using the particular database that you are accessing. (Instructions can usually be accessed from the home page of a database.) While all databases permit searches for publications that deal with particular keywords, many have special features (such as a search of titles only in *PsycINFO*) to assist users.

For more information on accessing these three databases plus the ones described in Appendix C, and consult the reference librarian at your college or university library.

Appendix B
Sample *ERIC* Search

Keywords: Child Language, Language Acquisition, and/or Cognitive Development

1. EJ653950. Matsuo, Ayumi; Duffield, Nigel. VP-Ellipsis and Anaphora in Child Language Acquisition. Language Acquisition; v9 n4 p301–27 2001.

2. EJ639697. Stephenson, Margaret E. "Homo Loquens": Language in the Context of Cosmic Education. NAMTA Journal; v26 n2 p83–96 Spr 2001.

3. EJ639698. Bickerton, Derek. Evolving Language: From Child to Human Species. NAMTA Journal; v26 n2 p99–119 Spr 2001.

4. EJ641771. Scholnick, Ellin Kofsky. Integration: An Agenda for Developmental Research. Monographs of the Society for Research in Child Development; v66 n4 p92–101 2001.

5. EJ637753. Crain-Thoreson, Catherine; Dahlin, Michael P.; Powell, Terris A. Parent-Child Interaction in Three Conversational Contexts: Variations in Style and Strategy. New Directions for Child and Adolescent Development; n92 p23–37 Sum 2001.

6. EJ626894. Gramlich, Jo Ann. Talking to Your Child. Montessori Life; v13 n1 p7 Win 2001.

7. EJ639694. Eliot, Lise. Language and the Developing Brain. NAMTA Journal; v26 n2 p8–60 Spr 2001.

8. EJ615368. Ely, Richard; MacGibbon, Ann; McCabe, Allyssa. "She Don't Care": Negatives in Children's Narratives. Merrill-Palmer Quarterly; v46 n3 p465–90 Jul 2000.

9. EJ605091. Myers-Scotton, Carol; Jake, Janice L. Testing the 4-M Model: Introduction. International Journal of Bilingualism; v4 n1 p1–8 Mar 2000.

10. EJ651055. Birch, Susan A. J.; Bloom, Paul. Preschoolers Are Sensitive to the Speaker's Knowledge When Learning Proper Names. Child Development; v73 n2 p434–44 Mar-Apr 2002.

11. EJ637755. Storch, Stacey A.; Whitehurst, Grover J. The Role of Family and Home in the Literacy Development of Children from Low-Income Backgrounds. New Directions for Child and Adolescent Development; n92 p53–71 Sum 2001.

12. EJ637754. Senechal, Monique; LeFevre, Jo-Anne. Storybook Reading and Parent Teaching: Links to Language and Literacy Development. New Directions for Child and Adolescent Development; n92 p39–52 Sum 2001.

13. EJ631059. Restrepo, Maria Adelaida; Gutierrez-Clellen, Vera F. Article Use in Spanish-Speaking Children with SLI. Journal of Child Language; v28 n2 p433–52 Jun 2001.

14. EJ643718. Ely, Richard; Gleason, Jean Berko; MacGibbon, Ann; Zaretsky, Elena. Attention to Language: Lessons Learned at the Dinner Table. Social Development; v10 n3 p355–73 2001.

15. EJ637756. Britto, Pia Rebello; Brooks-Gunn, Jeanne. Beyond Shared Book Reading: Dimensions of Home Literacy and Low-Income African American Preschoolers' Skills. New Directions for Child and Adolescent Development; n92 p73–89 Sum 2001.

16. EJ608583. Feldman, Heidi M.; Dollaghan, Christine A.; Campbell, Thomas F.; Kurs-Lasky, Marcia; Janosky, Janine E.; Paradise, Jack L. Measurement Properties of the MacArthur Communicative Development Inventories at Ages One and Two Years. [Journal title and dates are missing in *ERIC*.]

17. EJ635241. Crago, Martha B.; Allen, Shanley E. M. Early Finiteness in Inuktitut: The Role of Language Structure and Input. Language Acquisition; v9 n1 p59–111 2001.

18. EJ637797. Klein, Helen Altman. The World of Words: For Parents Particularly. Childhood Education; v77 n4 p234–35 Sum 2001.

19. EJ651054. Hoff, Erika; Naigles, Letitia. How Children Use Input to Acquire a Lexicon. Child Development; v73 n2 p418–33 Mar-Apr 2002.

20. EJ641171. Wijnen, Frank; Kempen, Masja; Gillis, Steven. Root Infinitives in Dutch Early Child Language: An Effect of Input? Journal of Child Language; v28 n3 p629–60 Oct 2001.

21. EJ628051. Rutherford, William; Thomas, Margaret. The "Child Language Data Exchange System" in Research on Second Language Acquisition. Second Language Research; v17 n2 p195–212 Apr 2001.

22. EJ646365. Taylor, Reid. Helping Language Grow. Instructor; v111 n6 p24–25 Mar 2002.

23. EJ641175. Levin, Iris; Ravid, Dorit; Rapaport, Sharon. Morphology and Spelling among Hebrew-Speaking Children: From Kindergarten to First Grade. Journal of Child Language; v28 n3 p741–72 Oct 2001.

24. EJ603926. MacNeilage, Peter F.; Davis, Barbara L.; Kinney, Ashlynn; Matyear, Christine L. The Motor Core of Speech: A Comparison of Serial Organization Patterns in Infants and Languages. 2000.

25. EJ616521. Kim, Young-Joo. Subject/Object Drop in the Acquisition of Korean: A Cross-Linguistic Comparison. Journal of East Asian Linguistics; v9 n4 p325–51 Oct 2000.

26. EJ641770. Bloom, Lois; Tinker, Erin. The Intentionality Model and Language Acquisition: Engagement, Effort, and the Essential Tension in Development. Monographs of the Society for Research in Child Development; v66 n4 p1–91 2001.

27. EJ631070. Snyder, William. On the Nature of Syntactic Variation: Evidence from Complex Predicates and Complex Word-Formation. Language; v77 n2 p324–42 Jun 2001.

28. EJ631045. Juan-Garau, Maria; Perez-Vidal, Carmen. Mixing and Pragmatic Parental Strategies in Early Bilingual Acquisition. Journal of Child Language; v28 n1 p59–86 Feb 2001.

29. EJ601625. Hua, Zhu; Dodd, Barbara. The Phonological Acquisition of Putonghua (Modern Standard Chinese). Journal of Child Language; v27 n1 p3–42 Feb 2000.

30. EJ639786. Jaffe, Joseph; Beebe, Beatrice; Feldstein, Stanley; Crown, Cynthia L.; Jasnow, Michael D. Rhythms of Dialogue in Infancy: Coordinated Timing in Development. Monographs of the Society for Research in Child Development; v66 n2 p1–132 2001.

31. EJ631057. Tam, Clara W.Y.; Stokes, Stephanie F. Form and Function of Negation in Early Developmental Cantonese. Journal of Child Language; v28 n2 p373–91 Jun 2001.

32. EJ631049. Thal, Donna J.; Flores, Melanie. Development of Sentence Interpretation Strategies by Typically Developing and Late-Talking Toddlers. Journal of Child Language; v28 n1 p173–93 Feb 2001.

33. EJ631044. Otomo, Kiyoshi. Maternal Responses to Word Approximations in Japanese Children's Transition to Language. Journal of Child Language; v28 n1 p29–57 Feb 2001.

34. EJ636449. Snow, Catherine E. Knowing What We Know: Children, Teachers, Researchers. Educational Researcher; v30 n7 p3–9 Oct 2001.

35. EJ609817. Kim, Mikyong; McGregor, Karla K.; Thompson, Cynthia K. Early Lexical Development in English- and Korean-Speaking Children: Language-General and Language-Specific Patterns. Journal of Child Language; v27 n2 p225–54 Jun 2000.

36. EJ631048. Goodluck, Helen; Terzi, Arhonto; Diaz, Gema Chocano. The Acquisition of Control Crosslinguistically: Structural and Lexical Factors in Learning to Licence PRO. Journal of Child Language; v28 n1 p153–72 Feb 2001.

37. EJ639693. Montanaro, Silvana. Language Acquisition. NAMTA Journal; v26 n2 p1–7 Spr 2001.

38. EJ637867. McCathren, Rebecca B. "How Language Comes to Children: From Birth to Two Years" by Benedicte de Boysson-Bardies, translated by M.B. DeBevoise. Book Review 2001.

39. EJ631060. Petitto, Laura Ann; Katerelos, Marina; Levy, Bronna G.; Gauna, Kristine; Tetreault, Karine; Ferraro, Vittoria. Bilingual Signed and Spoken Language Acquisition from Birth: Implications for the Mechanisms Underlying Early Bilingual Language Acquisition. [Date missing in *Eric*.]

40. EJ641176. Camaioni, Luigia; Longobardi, Emiddia. Noun versus Verb Emphasis in Italian Mother-to-Child Speech. Journal of Child Language; v28 n3 p773–86 Oct 2001.

41. EJ609854. Hestvik, Arild; Philip, William. Binding and Coreference in Norwegian Child Language. Language Acquisition; v8 n3 p171–235 1999–2000.

42. EJ631058. Kehoe, Margaret M.; Stoel-Gammon, Carol. Development of Syllable Structure in English-Speaking Children with Particular Reference to Rhymes. Journal of Child Language; v28 n2 p393–432 Jun 2001.

43. EJ641169. Bergen, Benjamin K. Nativization Processes in L1 Esperanto. Journal of Child Language; v28 n3 p575–95 Oct 2001.

44. EJ616490. Rescorla, Leslie; Dahlsgaard, Katherine; Roberts, Julie. Late-Talking Toddlers: MLU and IPSyn Outcomes at 3;0 and 4;0. Journal of Child Language; v27 n3 p643–64 Oct 2000.

45. EJ613090. Cowley, Stephen J. The Baby, the Bathwater, and the "Language Instinct" Debate. Language Sciences; v23 n1 p69–91 Jan 2001.

46. EJ631052. Dabrowska, Ewa; Demuth, Katherine; Dressler, Wolfgang U.; Kilani-Schoch, Marianne; Echols, Catharine H.; Leonard, Laurence B.; Lleo, Conxita; Lopez-Ornat, Susana; Menn, Lise; Feldman, Andrea; Radford, Andrew; Veneziano, Edy; Vihman, Marilyn May; Velleman. Commentaries on "Filler Syllables: What Is Their Status in Emerging Grammar?" [Title of journal missing in *ERIC*.]

47.   EJ631043. O'Neill, Daniela K.; Topolovec, Jane C. Two-Year-Old Children's Sensitivity to the Referential (In)efficacy of Their Own Pointing Gestures. Journal of Child Language; v28 n1 p1–28 Feb 2001.

48.   EJ601630. Rowland, Caroline F.; Pine, Julian M. Subject-Auxiliary Inversion Errors and Who Question Acquisition: What Children Do Know. Journal of Child Language; v27 n1 p157–81 Feb 2000.

49.   EJ652256. Hagstrom, Paul. Implications of Child Errors for the Syntax of Negation in Korean. Journal of East Asian Linguistics; v11 n3 p211–42 Jul 2002.

50.   EJ641170. Dinnsen, Daniel A.; O'Connor, Kathleen M. Typological Predictions in Developmental Phonology. Journal of Child Language; v28 n3 p597–628 Oct 2001.

51.   EJ641168. Dabrowska, Ewa. Learning a Morphological System without a Default: The Polish Genitive. Journal of Child Language; v28 n3 p545–74 Oct 2001.

52.   EJ609819. Parisse, Christophe; Le Normand, Marie-Therese. How Children Build Their Morphosyntax: The Case of French. Journal of Child Language; v27 n2 p267–92 Jun 2000.

53.   EJ631062. Schutze, Carson T. Productive Inventory and Case/Agreement Contingencies: A Methodological Note on Rispoli (1999). Journal of Child Language; v28 n2 p507–15 Jun 2001.

54.   EJ631054. Barlow, Jessica A. The Structure of /s/-Sequences: Evidence from a Disordered System. Journal of Child Language; v28 n2 p291–324 Jun 2001.

55.   EJ631050. Wong, Winnie W.Y.; Stokes, Stephanie F. Cantonese Consonantal Developmental: Towards a Nonlinear Account. Journal of Child Language; v28 n1 p195–212 Feb 2001.

56.   EJ631047. Theakston, Anna L.; Lieven, Elena V. M.; Pine, Julian M.; Rowland, Caroline F. The Role of Performance Limitations in the Acquisition of Verb–Argument Structure: An Alternative Account. 2001.

57.   EJ608584. Fenson, Larry; Bates, Elizabeth; Dale, Philip; Goodman, Judith; Reznick J., Steven; Thal, Donna. Measuring Variability in Early Child Language: Don't Shoot the Messenger. 2000.

58.   EJ643715. Locke, John L. First Communion: The Emergence of Vocal Relationships. Social Development; v10 n3 p294–308 2001.

59.   EJ645007. Lederer, Susan Hendler. Efficacy of Parent–Child Language Group Intervention for Late-Talking Toddlers: Infant–Toddler Intervention. The Transdisciplinary Journal; v11 n3–4 p223–35 Sep-Dec 2001.

60.   EJ641172. Wagner, Laura. Aspectual Influences on Early Tense Comprehension. Journal of Child Language; v28 n3 p661–81 Oct 2001.

61.   EJ616489. Dale, Philip S.; Ginette, Dionne; Eley, Thalia C.; Plomin, Robert. Lexical and Grammatical Development: A Behavioural Genetic Perspective. Journal of Child Language; v27 n3 p619–42 Oct 2000.

62.   EJ609820. Rescorla, Leslie; Mirak, Jennifer; Singh, Leher. Vocabulary Growth in Late Talkers: Lexical Development from 2.0 to 3.0. Journal of Child Language; v27 n2 p293–311 Jun 2000.

63.   EJ631061. Goldman, Herbert I. Parental Reports of "MAMA" Sounds in Infants: An Exploratory Study. Journal of Child Language; v28 n2 p497–506 Jun 2001.

64.   EJ631051. Peters, Ann M. Filler Syllables: What Is Their Status in Emerging Grammar? Journal of Child Language; v28 n1 p229–42 Feb 2001.

65.   EJ635072. Gilger, Jeffrey W.; Ho, Hsiu-Zu; Whipple, Angela D.; Spitz, Romy. Genotype–Environment Correlations for Language-Related Abilities: Implications for Typical and Atypical Learners. Journal of Learning Disabilities; v34 n6 p492–502 Nov-Dec 2001.

66.   EJ645838. Tayler, Collette. Australian Early Childhood Milieu: Teacher Challenges in Promoting Children's Language and Thinking. European Early Childhood Education Research Journal; v9 n1 p41–56 2001.

67.   EJ639787. Rochat, Philippe. Dialogical Nature of Cognition. Monographs of the Society for Research in Child Development; v66 n2 p133–43 2001.

68.   EJ606653. Guasti, Maria Teresa; Chierchia, Gennaro. Backward versus Forward Anaphora: Reconstruction in Child Grammar. Language Acquisition; v8 n2 p129–70 1999–2000.

69.   EJ605125. Kehoe, Margaret M. Truncation without Shape Constraints: The Latter Stages of Prosodic Acquisition. Language Acquisition; v8 n1 p23–67 1999–2000.

70.   EJ630927. Keshavarz, Mohammad Hossein. Halliday's Communicative–Functional Model Revisited: A Case Study. Communication Disorders Quarterly; v22 n4 p187–96 Sum 2001.

71.   EJ644230. Waxman, Sandra R.; Booth, Amy E. Seeing Pink Elephants: Fourteen-Month-Olds' Interpretations of Novel Nouns and Adjectives. Cognitive Psychology; v43 n3 p217–42 Nov 2001.

72.   EJ641177. Deak, Gedeon O.; Yen, Loulee; Pettit, Jeremy. By Any Other Name: When Will Preschoolers Produce Several Labels for a Referent? Journal of Child Language; v28 n3 p787–804 Oct 2001.

73.   EJ616484. Veneziano, Edy; Sinclair, Hermine. The Changing Status of "Filler Syllables" on the Way to Grammatical Morphemes. Journal of Child Language; v27 n3 p461–500 Oct 2000.

74. EJ609826. Huang, Chiung-Chih. Temporal Reference in Chinese Mother–Child Conversation: Morphosyntactic, Semantic, and Discourse-Pragmatic Resources. Journal of Child Language; v27 n2 p421–35 Jun 2000.

75. EJ631064. Lee, Elizabeth A.; Torrance, Nancy; Olson, David R. Young Children and the Say/Mean Distinction: Verbatim and Paraphrase Recognition in Narrative and Nursery Rhyme Contexts. Journal of Child Language; v28 n2 p531–43 Jun 2001.

76. EJ631063. Maas, Fay K.; Abbeduto, Leonard J. Children's Judgments about Intentionally and Unintentionally Broken Promises. Journal of Child Language; v28 n2 p517–29 Jun 2001.

77. EJ631056. D'Odorico, Laura; Carubbi, Stefania; Salerni, Nicoletta; Calvo, Vicenzo. Vocabulary Development in Italian Children: A Longitudinal Evaluation of Quantitative and Qualitative Aspects. 2001.

78. EJ631055. Kelly, Spencer D. Broadening the Units of Analysis in Communication: Speech and Nonverbal Behaviours in Pragmatic Comprehension. Journal of Child Language; v28 n2 p325–49 Jun 2001.

79. EJ631053. Peters, Ann M. Response to Comments. Journal of Child Language; v28 n1 p283–89 Feb 2001.

80. EJ631046. Gathercole, Virginia C. Mueller; Whitfield, Lisa Cramer. Function as a Criterion for the Extension of New Words. Journal of Child Language; v28 n1 p87–125 Feb 2001.

81. EJ601631. Maratsos, Michael. More Overregularizations after All: New Data and Discussion on Marcus, Pinker, Ullman, Hollander, Rosen, and Xu. Journal of Child Language; v27 n1 p183–212 Feb 2000.

82. EJ635766. Selman, Ruth. Talk Time: Programming Communicative Interaction into the Toddler Day. Young Children; v56 n3 p15–18 May 2001.

83. EJ616486. Bassano, Dominique. Early Development of Nouns and Verbs in French: Exploring the Interface between Lexicon and Grammar. Journal of Child Language; v27 n3 p521–59 Oct 2000.

84. EJ629575. Dinnsen, Daniel A.; McGarrity, Laura W.; O'Connor, Kathleen M.; Swanson, Kimberly A. B. On the Role of Sympathy in Acquisition. Language Acquisition; v8 n4 p321–61 1999–2000.

85. EJ641173. Gelman, Susan A.; Koenig, Melissa A. The Role of Animacy in Children's Understanding of "Move." Journal of Child Language; v28 n3 p683–701 Oct 2001.

86. EJ639307. Grinstead, John. Wh-Movement in Child Catalan. Issues in Applied Linguistics; v12 n1 p5–28 Jun 2001.

87. EJ629547. Wong, Andrew D. Explicit Introductions in Lexical Acquisition: A Case Study. Issues in Applied Linguistics; v11 n2 p149–74 Dec 2000.

88. EJ616488. Lakshmanan, Usha. The Acquisition of Relative Clauses by Tamil Children. Journal of Child Language; v27 n3 p587–617 Oct 2000.

89. EJ616485. Goldfield, Beverly A. Nouns Before Verbs in Comprehension versus Production: The View from Pragmatics. Journal of Child Language; v27 n3 p501–20 Oct 2000.

90. EJ648979. Gavruseva, Elena; Thornton, Rosalind. Getting It Right: Acquisition of "Whose"-Questions in Child English. Language Acquisition; v9 n3 p229–67 2001.

91. EJ641174. Tsang, Kitty, K. S.; Stokes, Stephanie F. Syntactic Awareness of Cantonese-Speaking Children. Journal of Child Language; v28 n3 p703–39 Oct 2001.

92. EJ639771. Childers, Jane B.; Tomasello, Michael. The Role of Pronouns in Young Children's Acquisition of the English Transitive Construction. Developmental Psychology; v37 n6 p739–48 Nov 2001.

93. EJ637776. Brent, Michael R.; Siskind, Jeffrey M. The Role of Exposure to Isolated Words in Early Vocabulary Development. Cognition; v81 n2 pB33–B44 Sep 2001.

94. EJ637228. Girolametto, Luigi; Weitzman, Elaine; van Lieshout, Riet; Duff, Dawna. Directiveness in Teachers' Language Input to Toddlers and Preschoolers in Day Care. Journal of Speech, Language, and Hearing Research; v43 n5 p1101–14 Oct 2000.

95. EJ649419. Mintz, Toben H.; Gleitman, Lila R. Adjectives Really Do Modify Nouns: The Incremental and Restricted Nature of Early Adjective Acquisition. Cognition; v84 n3 p267–93 Jul 2002.

96. EJ643717. Smiley, Patricia A. Intention Understanding and Partner-Sensitive Behaviors in Young Children's Peer Interactions. Social Development; v10 n3 p330–54 2001.

97. EJ605473. Ryalls, Brigette Oliver. Dimensional Adjectives: Factors Affecting Children's Ability to Compare Objects Using Novel Words. Journal of Experimental Child Psychology; v76 n1 p26–49 May 2000.

98. EJ635642. de Haan, Dorian; Singer, Elly. Young Children's Language of Togetherness. International Journal of Early Years Education; v9 n2 p117–24 Jun 2001.